Business Builder

Intermediate Teacher's Resource

Modules 7, 8, 9

- Presentations

- Company, products and customer relations

- Negotiations

 *Paul Emmerson*

Contents

Introduction

Needs Analysis

8.7	**Competitive advantage** Company strengths: procedures, product quality, after-sales.	40-50	Skills Practice
8.8	**Market profile for consumer products** Target market and buying behaviour of consumers.	40-50	Skills Practice
8.9	**Selling mobile phones** Customer/supplier sales conversation: features, price, terms of payment.	40-50	Skills Practice
8.10	**Selling your products on the telephone** Sales conversation based on students' own products.	50-60	Skills Practice
8.11	**Apologize, explain and offer** Making and dealing with complaints.	50-60	Skills Practice
8.12	**Dialogue building: selling your products** Open framework for writing a sales conversation.	variable	Skills Practice
8.13	**Dialogue building: complaining and apologizing** Open framework for writing a complaining dialogue.	variable	Skills Practice

Negotiations

		Minutes	Activity type
9.1	**An introduction to negotiating** Negotiating vocabulary. Students' own negotiations.	30-40	Language Work
9.2	**Opening the negotiation** Relationship-building, discussing needs and starting positions.	40-50	Language Work
9.3	**Bargaining and closing** Making and reacting to proposals, closing a negotiation.	50-60	Language Work
9.4	**Tentative language** could/would, opening phrases, negative questions, qualifiers. Use of tentative language.	40-50	Language Work
9.5	**Negotiating tactics** Being open or specific, linking issues, increasing/decreasing the value of concessions.	30-40	Language Work
9.6	**Checking understanding and summarizing** Asking for clarification, paraphrasing, summarizing. Clarifying what you said.	40-50	Language Work
9.7	**The negotiating process** Personal effectiveness, difficulties, tactics. Planning a forthcoming negotiation.	40-50	Skills Practice
9.8	**Computers** Customer/supplier negotiation: quantity, price, exclusivity, terms of payment.	50-60	Skills Practice
9.9	**Lamps** Customer/supplier negotiation: choice of product, price, additional services.	50-60	Skills Practice
9.10	**A salary increase** Employee/manager negotiation: salary increase and benefits.	40-50	Skills Practice
9.11	**Generation gap** Teenager/parent negotiation: dealing with difficult people and conflicts of interest.	30-40	Skills Practice
9.12	**Dialogue building: real-life negotiation** Open framework for writing a negotiating dialogue.	variable	Skills Practice

Introduction

Business Builder

Business Builder is a collection of photocopiable activities for teaching business communication skills. It uses a 'mix and match' approach: you customize the course to the needs of your students. The full range of business skills is covered by three Teacher's Resource Books:

- Modules 1, 2, 3. Social English; Telephoning; Job interviews

- Modules 4, 5, 6. Discussions and meetings; Business correspondence; Business reports

- Modules 7, 8, 9. Presentations; Company, products and customer relations; Negotiations

A further component is **Business Grammar Builder** by Paul Emmerson and Michael Vince (Macmillan Heinemann). This is a student workbook with grammar explanations and practice exercises set in a business context. It also contains a reference section with key phrases and 'How to' hints for all business skills.

Level

All activities are designed for Intermediate students. Many of the skills practice activities work well with Pre-intermediate and Upper-intermediate students as well.

One-to-one

Most of the activities are suitable for one-to-one lessons.

Needs Analysis

At the beginning of each Teacher's Resource Book is a Needs Analysis sheet. (See Teacher's Notes for Worksheet 8.1 for a suggested lesson that includes the Needs Analysis.) Treat any course programme flexibly and review it at regular intervals.

The Needs Analysis has three sections. For 'Communication skills' use Business Builder. For 'Business topics' use a mixture of authentic articles from newspapers/magazines for selection and recording of useful vocabulary and discussion; vocabulary exercises from published books; student presentations; and in-company material provided by the students. For 'Grammar' use diagnostic feedback from skills activities followed up by exercises from **Business Grammar Builder**.

Cultural hints

The Teacher's Notes contain occasional sections labelled 'Cultural hints'. These give background information on business styles in different cultures.

Speaking activities

The Teacher's Notes refer to doing pairwork activities twice, with students swapping roles and/or partners the second time. This is important: the second time is often more productive for both language practice and business content. Take notes during a role-play for later feedback. After a role-play allow the students to de-role by discussing the content and outcome of the activity, then look at both good and poor language use.

Feedback slots

The Teacher's Notes refer to 'feedback slots', and you should always allow time for feedback and correction after speaking activities. Doing language work through feedback allows you to start with real problems and needs revealed by a particular group in a particular activity. Your role here is one of Language Consultant.

Remember that business students are usually more interested in clear, effective communication than in high levels of grammatical accuracy or rarely needed native-speaker collocations. Give students the opportunity to correct or reformulate themselves before you make suggestions. Write vocabulary and grammar examples on the board as part of whole phrases that show a clear context.

Choose a variety of areas for feedback: vocabulary, useful collocations, grammar, functional phrases and pronunciation.

Pronunciation work is a very important part of feedback. Important areas for business English are likely to be: pronunciation and word stress of individual words; emphasizing key words in a phrase; and polite, friendly intonation. Provide a model yourself and use choral/individual repetition to give students a chance to practise making the new sounds.

Needs Analysis

You and your job

Which company do you work for?

_____

What is their main area of business?

_____

What is your position in the company?

_____

What do you do?

_____

Communication skills

How much time do you want to spend on different communication skills on this course?
Circle a number, from 0 (no time) to 4 (a lot of time).

Discussions and meetings	0	1	2	3	4	_____
Telephoning	0	1	2	3	4	_____
Social English	0	1	2	3	4	_____
Company, products and customer relations	0	1	2	3	4	_____
Presentations	0	1	2	3	4	_____
Negotiating	0	1	2	3	4	_____
Business correspondence	0	1	2	3	4	_____
Business reports	0	1	2	3	4	_____
Job interviews	0	1	2	3	4	_____

Now give more details about each skill. Who do you communicate with in English? What about?
Make notes on the lines above, next to the appropriate skills.

Business topics

Which topics are you interested in? Choose from the list below. You can add another topic of
your own at the end.

Management ☐   **Production** ☐   **Political/economic context** ☐   **Travel** ☐

Sales and marketing ☐   **Human resources** ☐   **International trade** ☐   **Entertaining** ☐

Finance ☐   **New technology** ☐   **Recent business news** ☐   _____ ☐

Grammar

How much grammar have you studied before coming on this course? _____

How much grammar would you like to do on this course? Any particular areas? _____

Other objectives

Do you have any other objectives for this course that you have not mentioned?

_____

_____

Is there anything else you would like to tell your teacher to help him/her to plan your course?

_____

_____

7.1a

An introduction to presentations

AIM

To discuss presentation structure and techniques and consider two alternative openings.

TIME

40–50 minutes

PREPARATION

Make one copy of the worksheet (two pages) for each student in the class.

PROCEDURE

1 Write up on the board the heading *Presentation structure*, and underneath the seven words in the box from section A in random order. Elicit the meaning of each one in the context of presentations (Bang! = something that makes people pay attention; Recap = recapitulate/review/summarize; Bridge = a connection between the presentation and the needs of the audience). Write the numbers 1 to 7 at the bottom of the board, divide the class into pairs, and ask students to decide what is a typical order for the different stages. Take class feedback, focussing on the range of possibilities rather than any single correct answer (section A of the worksheet will provide a possible sequence).

2 Give out a copy of the worksheet to every student and ask them to look at **section A**. Refer to the instructions. Divide the class into pairs, start the activity and circulate.

ANSWERS

1 Bang! 2 Opening 3 Message 4 Bridge
5 Examples 6 Recap 7 Bang!

3 Refer to the instructions for **section B**. Divide the class into pairs, start the activity and circulate.

ANSWERS

1 Opening (c) 2 Final Bang! 3 First Bang!
4 Bridge (or Message) 5 Recap
6 Opening (a and b)

A Study the stages of a presentation 1–7. Then fill in the gaps with words from the box below.

1 Start with something to get attention: a surprising fact; a reference to 'here and now'; a question; a humorous quote/story; audience participation; a visual aid. _____

2 a) Say a few words about yourself b) Tell the audience the structure of your talk c) Tell the audience how they will benefit from your presentation. _____

3 Present a small number of main points – a maximum of four. _____

4 Connect each point to the needs/interests of your audience. For example, show the audience how they will benefit or ask them a question. _____

5 Give examples to make your points clear. _____

6 Summarize the main points again. Mention the key benefits – how audience members can apply the information in your talk to their specific situation. _____

7 Finish with impact: a link back to your opening Bang!; a dramatic statement which sums up your message; an unusual visual aid; a strong *Thank you for your attention*; a call to action (something you want the audience to do). _____

Examples   Recap   Bang!   Bang!   Bridge   Message   Opening

B The first letters of the answers you wrote in Section A spell 'BOMBER B'. Remember this phrase – it will help you to plan your presentations. Match each extract below with a stage of BOMBER B.

1 By the end of my talk you will be able to decide if you need to …, and if so what are the different options.
Opening (c)

2 OK, let's stop there. I'd like to finish by thanking you all for your attention. I'm now going to distribute this brochure …. As you can see from the title, the message I want to leave you with today is: 'Let's grow – together.' _____

3 Well, good morning everyone. I hope you all found somewhere to park your car this morning. They say the roadworks will be finished shortly, but they've been saying that for the past six months! OK, today I'm going to talk to you about a new product to help people to give up smoking. Did you know that every day 1,000 people die from smoking-related diseases? That's the same as two jumbo jets crashing every day. _____

4 I'd like to turn to the question of …. How many of your clients put this as their number one priority? _____

5 Right, I think that covers everything. So, before I finish, let me just summarize my main points again. I've talked about …, I also described …, and I explained …. In short, I've tried to show you how … _____

6 My name is … and I'm a Senior Partner here at Morris Brothers. During my presentation I'll be talking about three main areas. First, I'll tell you a little about …, second …, and third why we believe we can offer …. If anyone has any questions, please feel free to interrupt. _____

4 Refer to the instructions for **section C**. First ask the students to read the two alternatives silently, then choose two students to read the openings aloud. Elicit the basic difference between the openings (Opening 1 is more traditional and formal, perhaps more European. Opening 2 is more spontaneous and informal, perhaps more American). Develop a class discussion on the three points at the end of the section.

POSSIBLE ANSWERS

1 *Opening 1: advantages and disadvantages*
   - ✓ It is safer for a non-native speaker because it is clear and simple
   - ✓ It relies less on personality
   - ✓ It guarantees that all the important points will be covered
   - ✓ It makes the structure clear at the beginning
   - ✓ It tells the audience when to ask questions
   - ✗ It might be boring
   - ✗ It might tell the audience what they already know

2 *Opening 2: advantages and disadvantages*
   - ✓ It is lively and involves the audience immediately
   - ✓ It is flexible: the speaker can find out and deal with what the audience is interested in
   - ✓ It uses visual humor and simple transparencies that make an impact
   - ✗ It is risky for non-native speakers
   - ✗ It relies on a strong, extrovert personality
   - ✗ The speaker might lose direction or miss important points

3 Opening 1 might be better in-company; where the context is more formal; and when doing factual, non-sales presentations. Opening 2 might be better where the context is more informal and for sales presentations.

5 Refer to **section D** and develop a class discussion on the eight points.

POSSIBLE ANSWERS

1 Reading word for word is boring. It is difficult to maintain contact with the audience. You cannot see people's reactions. The alternatives are to write down main points only (e.g. on cards) or use your transparencies as your guide.

2 An amazing fact, a provocative opinion, a humorous story, a quote, audience participation, a visual aid. 'Here and now' references work well: the coffee, the room, the weather, something in the comments of the person who introduced you, something that happened the last time you were here etc.

3 A good technique is: Pause, breathe slowly and deeply, look around the audience, smile.

4 Yes. It is easier to absorb the main points if you are told the overall structure first. Also it shows that the speaker is in control and has practised the talk.

5 Yes. It reinforces the message.

6 Questions during the presentation:
   - more spontaneous and lively
   - allow you to respond to the interests of the group.
   - a danger of losing direction or missing points .
   Questions at the end:
   - better for large groups
   - better when the content is factual and needs to be covered comprehensively.
   - a danger that you may tell the audience what they already know.

7 Typical aids include transparencies on the OHP (overhead projector), flipchart, slides, computer-generated presentations using a projector and remote mouse/laser pointer.

8 Develop a class discussion.

6 (Option) At this point you may want students to give a very short presentation (5 mins.) to break the ice. Explain that they will have a chance to practise longer presentations related to their work later in the course. Write on the board some possible topics:
   - *Why you should visit my city/country*
   - *A comparison of two cultures/companies I know*
   - *My hobby*
   - *Own choice*

Allow two minutes only for preparation, and ask students to simply write down two or three main points and look again at BOMBER B. Ask students to give their presentations, and encourage a few questions at the end of each one. Make a note of good/bad language use. Hold a short feedback slot.

CULTURAL HINTS

▼ In America the presenter usually has a more informal style and gives a 'hard sell'. Modern audiovisual aids are used and the aim is maximum impact. The audience may ask questions or interrupt while someone is speaking.

▼ In Britain the presenter often has a more formal style and uses humour and an appeal to tradition. Germans like a presentation with technical details about the product and no jokes. The French like a formal, logical approach mixed with imagination.

▼ In Latin America and southern Europe presentations are lively and eloquent. The opening includes appreciation of hospitality. Comments are directed to the senior person. Much use is made of hands and body language to emphasize a point. Audience members may want a more personal 'extra' talk afterwards.

▼ In Japan and south-east Asia the audience likes facts and data rather than abstract concepts. The opening is formal and includes appreciation of hospitality. Comments are directed to everyone. The Japanese ask repeated questions to check understanding.

Read these alternative openings for a presentation on renting office space. Notice that the content of the two openings is basically the same.

Opening 1

Good morning, ladies and gentlemen. First of all, I'd like to thank you for inviting me here to speak to you today, and I hope that after that excellent coffee no one will fall asleep during my presentation! Well, let me introduce myself – my name is Carlos Pinto and I am the Sales Director of Centre-Space Properties.

My objective here today is to help you to find the right office for your business. During my talk I'll be looking at four areas. (*looks briefly at notes*) I'll begin by introducing our company, then I'll show you some slides of office space that we have available in this city. After that I'll move on to describe our optional service package, which includes security and secretarial services. Finally, I'll deal with the question of price. My presentation will take around 20 minutes, and if you have any questions I'll be pleased to answer them at the end.

OK. (*shows slide with an organigram of the company*) Let's start by looking at who we are and how the company has developed over the last 10 years.

Opening 2

I bet you're sick of looking for office space, right? Are you feeling like this? (*shows slide of a confused businessman in a small room with a big question mark over his head*) Who feels like that? (*looks around room, everyone laughs*) Wouldn't you prefer to feel like this? (*shows slide of a relaxed executive in a large office with plants and a line of clients in the background*)

You all know the importance of location for business success. Well, we can help you. (*shows transparency with a few words in large print*) My company is called Centre-Space Properties. Our success over 10 years has been built on a simple philosophy. We offer our clients: (*pointing to words on slide*) choice; an optional service package for your complete business needs; and the right price.

Right, I'd like to begin with a question: do you know which area in this city has the highest rent costs per square metre? (*looks round, waiting for answer*)

Discuss:

1 What are the advantages and disadvantages of opening 1?
2 What are the advantages and disadvantages of opening 2?
3 Can you think of situations where each would be appropriate?

D Discuss these points:

1 What is the problem with reading a presentation word for word? What alternatives are there?
2 How can you 'break the ice' at the beginning of a presentation?
3 What techniques can the presenter use to relax if he/she starts to feel nervous?
4 Is it a good idea to tell the audience at the beginning what you will talk about and for how long?
5 Is it a good idea to summarize the main points again at the end?
6 Some people prefer to answer questions during their presentation, others at the end. What are the advantages and disadvantages of both methods?
7 What kind of audio-visual aids do you use in your presentations?
8 Can you give any other advice on how to give a successful presentation?

AIM

To practise language that refers to the structure of a presentation including: referring to the main points at the beginning, moving on, digressing, summarizing and concluding.

TIME

30–40 minutes

PREPARATION

Make one copy of the worksheet (two pages) for each student in the class.

PROCEDURE

1 Lead in to the example presentation by eliciting the names of some up-market watch brands (Rolex, Patek Philippe). Ask the students to imagine that they are giving a sales presentation for one of these brands to managers of a retail chain – what would they talk about? Brainstorm some ideas on to the board (*design of watch face, image, technology, battery, strap, material, water resistance, price, availability of promotional material, etc.*).

2 Give out a copy of the worksheet to every student and ask them to look at **section A**. Refer to the instructions. Let the students read through the presentation silently first, checking to see which of the brainstormed ideas are mentioned. Then ask one student to stand at the front of the class and read the extract slowly and clearly. Finally refer to the instructions and task after the extract. Divide the class into pairs, start the activity and circulate.

ANSWERS (BY PARAGRAPH)

I'm going to talk to you today about ... / I'll talk about ...

So, let's start by looking at ... / OK, that's all I want to say about ... / Any questions so far?

Right, let's move on to ... / Before going on, I'd just like to mention that ...

OK, finally I'd like to turn to ...

So, to sum up, I have talked about three main areas. First, ... second, ... and third, ... / I also mentioned ...

Right, let's stop there. / And now, if anyone has any questions, I'd be happy to try to answer them.

A In this presentation extract the speaker is trying to persuade the managers of a large retail chain to stock Reiko watches. Read the extract.

<u>I'm going to talk to you today about</u> Reiko watches. I'll talk about the technology that goes into a Reiko, the design of a Reiko, and, of course, the image of our watches in the market.

So, let's start by looking at the technology. Our new range of watches features a technological miracle. We have replaced the battery with a very small generator that makes its own electrical power by the movements of your hand. It's ecological, reliable and efficient: wear it one day to gain energy for at least two weeks. And all our watches are made of titanium – a light material, yet strong and kind to your skin. ..... OK, that's all I want to say about the technical details. Any questions so far?

Right, let's move on to the design and style of a Reiko. Every Reiko watch combines classical elegance with modern design. It represents both tradition and innovation. And our market research department makes sure that every generation of watches uses the latest style, the style that the customer really wants. ..... Before going on, I'd just like to mention that of course we support retailers who stock our products with a full range of promotional material such as counter displays, window displays and posters. I have some examples here to show you.

OK, finally I'd like to turn to the most important point: the image of our watches, and the feeling that our customers have when they wear one. As you know, Reiko watches are not cheap, but people who buy a Reiko are not looking for a cheap product. They are looking for something special, for something that gives confidence and represents the status they have achieved. To put it simply, they are looking for the best.

So, to sum up, I have talked about three main areas. First, the sophisticated modern technology that goes into a Reiko watch, second, the design of a Reiko that is based on the most up-to-date market research, and third, the image of a Reiko. I also mentioned the promotional support that we offer to retailers.

Right, let's stop there. Thank you very much for your attention. And now, if anyone has any questions, I'd be happy to try to answer them.

When you are on a journey, signposts show the direction you are going, where you are now, and where you have been.

In a presentation, signposts are short phrases that help the audience to follow the direction and structure of what you are saying. They are not part of the main information. Underline all the examples you can find in the extract above. The first one has been done for you.

3 Refer to the instructions for **section B**. Divide the class into pairs, start the activity and circulate. (Vocabulary note: 'to side-track' = 'to discuss something that is not relevant to the main topic'. Explain it with a drawing of a mountain, a main track and a side-track that leaves and then returns to the main track).

ANSWERS

1 **a** (on worksheet)   **b** Before going on, I'd just like to mention that ...   **c** finally I'd like to turn to ...
   d to sum up   **e** Right, let's stop there.
2 **a** move on to   **b** talk about   **c** deal with
   d cover   **e** look at   **f** explain   **g** consider
   h mention   **i** turn to
3 come back to

4 Refer to the instructions for **section C**. Divide the class into pairs, start the activity and circulate.

ANSWERS

1 e   **2** h   **3** a   **4** g   **5** c   **6** f   **7** b   **8** d

5 (Option) Students prepare and give a very short presentation (5 mins.). Explain that the objective is to practise signpost language, and so on this occasion they can deliberately exaggerate its use. Write on the board some possible topics:
– *A sales presentation of any object in the room*
– *What I like about my job*
– *Own choice*
Allow a few minutes for preparation, but emphasize that students should only write down two or three main points. Remind them of the five minute time limit for the presentation. Ask students to give their presentations in turn, and encourage a few questions at the end of each one. Make a note of good/bad language use. Hold a short feedback slot.

B Answer these questions

1 Find phrases in section A that are similar to the following.
   a Let's move on to the first point by …   *So, let's start by looking at*
   b If I can just side-track for a moment, …   _____
   c To conclude, I'd like to deal with …   _____
   d To summarize   _____
   e OK, I think that covers everything.   _____

2 *'I'd now like to discuss the question of cost.'* The words below can all replace 'discuss'. Fill in the missing vowels.
   a m_v_ _n t_   b t_lk _b_t   c d_l w_th   d c_v_r   e l__k _t
   f _xpl__n   g c_ns_d_r   h m_nt__n   i t_rn t_

3 When referring back you can say: 'I'd just like to go back for a moment to the previous slide.'
   When referring forward you can say: 'I'll _ _ _ _   _ _ _ _   _ _ this again later.'

C Put phrases a–h in the right place in the diagram below. The position of the arms will help you.

   a Secondly, I'd like to consider …
   b So, just before I finish, let me summarize the main points again. First, …, second, …, and finally, …
   c Before going on, I'd just like to take a moment to explain …
   d Right, let's stop there. If you have any questions, I'd be pleased to try to answer them.
   e I've divided my talk into three main parts. First I'll talk about …, then I'll mention …, and finally I'll say a little about …
   f To conclude, I'd like to deal briefly with …
   g As I mentioned earlier, …
   h OK, let's move on to the first point.

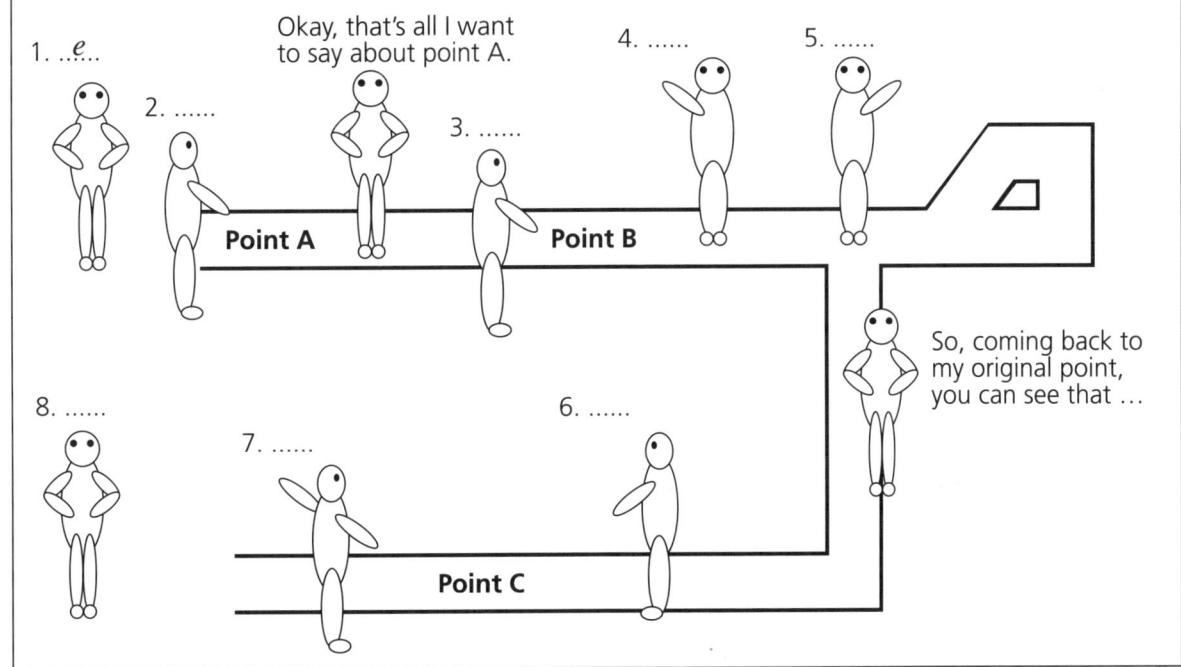

1. ..*e*..
2. ......
3. ......
4. ......
5. ......
6. ......
7. ......
8. ......

Point A
Point B
Point C

Okay, that's all I want to say about point A.

So, coming back to my original point, you can see that …

7.3
Using your voice

AIM

To practise the use of pauses (phonological chunking), emphasizing key ideas (sentence stress) and packaging ideas (intonation) in delivering an effective presentation.

TIME

30–40 minutes

PREPARATION

Make one copy of the worksheet for each student in the class.

PROCEDURE

1 Write up on the board *Using your voice to give a good presentation*. Elicit ideas from the students and write them on the board. Initial ideas might include speaking slowly and clearly, but elicit also the importance of pausing (to break up the information) and sentence stress (to emphasize important words).

2 Give out a copy of the worksheet to every student and ask them to look at **section A**. Refer to the instructions. Read the extract aloud three times yourself: the first time emphasize the pauses; the second time use your hand to beat the sentence stress as you read; the third time use your hand to trace the marked intonation pattern in the air as you read (the right way round for the students). Then go through the extract again chunk by chunk, modelling yourself with choral repetition from the students. You may find that your natural stress or intonation is slightly different to that marked on the sheet. This is quite normal and you should follow what is natural for you.

3 Now ask the students to stand up, spread out in the room, and practise reading aloud by themselves. They do this individually, standing up, but should start at different times/places in the text to avoid a chorus of voices in unison. Students may prefer to work on one thing at a time: first pausing, then emphasizing key words, then the intonation at the end of the phrase. Circulate and help. As a round-up, ask students to sit down again and ask one student to go to the front of the class and read the paragraph.

4 Refer to instructions 1–3 for **section B**. Ask students if there will be one right answer for this activity (no – even native speakers would pause in different places and say it differently on different occasions). Divide the class into pairs, start the activity and circulate. Monitor very closely and encourage students to say the phrases aloud to each other several times in different ways to see which sounds best. Take class feedback when they finish.

POSSIBLE ANSWERS

As you know, // we specialize in electrical distribution systems, // and our company // is well-known // for having the widest product range in the market. // The key philosophy // behind our products // is ease of assembly, // and indeed // we are regarded // as the leader in this field. // Our product system remains totally flexible // until the final installation // at the construction site. // And where are the construction sites? // You'll find our products // in every type of property, // from residential developments and office blocks // to factories and industrial units.

5 Ask students to follow instruction 4 individually. They stand up and spread out round the room, then read aloud by themselves again. Circulate and help, encouraging students to use their voices with greater range and variety. As a round-up, ask students to sit down and then ask one or two students to go to the front of the class and read the paragraph.

6 (Homework) Use **section C** as a homework option. After marking pauses, stress and intonation for section C, students can then practise reading aloud the whole presentation, sections A–C. Listen to some in the next class, and remind students to think about using their voice more effectively in all future presentations on the course.

CULTURAL HINTS

▼ Americans and Germans use a strong, unemotional voice. Most northern Europeans use a moderate tone of voice.

▼ Latin Americans and southern Europeans have a forceful, animated style which is believed to project sincerity.

▼ Asians have a quiet, restrained style. The Japanese use silence to establish harmony and sense the mood of the audience.

7.3
Using your voice

A To make your presentation interesting and easy to understand you must use your voice well. Listen to your teacher read this first extract from a presentation, then practise reading it yourself.

Good morning ladies and gentlemen. // I'm very glad to be here today // to have the chance // to tell you about our company. // Our company was founded // in nineteen fifty eight // as a small family business. // Today it employs // more than four hundred and sixty people, // and it has an annual turnover // of two hundred million dollars. // What are the reasons // for this outstanding growth? // The reasons are: // the quality of our products, // our attention to the needs of our customers, // and our decentralized management structure. // This structure allows: // flexibility, // motivation // and the rapid development of new ideas.

B Now follow this procedure for the paragraph in the box below from the same presentation.

1 <u>Decide where you would pause and put a // symbol</u>. Pauses allow you to break the information into small pieces that the audience can understand more easily.
2 <u>Underline the syllables that have a strong stress</u>. Inside each phrase you have marked there will be some syllables with a strong beat. Important words will always have a strongly stressed syllable.
3 <u>Check if there are any words that are difficult to say</u>. If there are, write the phonetic script with the help of a dictionary or put a ■ symbol above a stressed syllable.

> As you know, we specialize in electrical distribution systems, and our company is well-known for having the widest product range in the market. The key philosophy behind our products is ease of assembly, and indeed we are regarded as the leader in this field. Our product system remains totally flexible until the final installation at the construction site. And where are the construction sites? You'll find our products in every type of property, from residential developments and office blocks to factories and industrial units.

4 <u>Practise reading the text several times</u>. Use your voice to make the information as clear as possible. There are three main things to practise:
- Pausing at the // symbols so that the message has maximum impact. Practice pausing for two seconds, because this will help you to make pausing into a habit.
- Emphasizing key words by pausing just before them, or saying them with more force, or more slowly, or with a higher voice.
- Using the intonation of your voice to show if an idea is finished: a fall-rise at the end of a phrase shows the idea is not yet finished, a fall at the end shows it is.

C Follow the same procedure 1–4 for the next paragraph from the same presentation.

> OK, that's all I want to say about our product range. Now I'd like to say a few words about our market. Who exactly are our customers? Well, we sell more than seventy percent of our products through wholesalers, and the rest directly to builders. I'd also like to remind you that more than thirty percent of our production goes for export. We view our customers not just as customers – we view them as partners. Partners who can work with us to innovate and set new standards for electrical distribution systems.

▶ **PHOTOCOPIABLE**

7.4

Dealing with questions

AIM
To practise the techniques of clarifying and redirecting when answering questions.

TIME
50–60 minutes

PREPARATION
Make one copy of the worksheet for each student in the class.

PROCEDURE

1 Write up on the board *Dealing with questions* and ask students how they would deal with someone who asked a difficult question at the end of a presentation. Elicit and write on the board some possible techniques (*ask for clarification, redirect to the questioner/group*).

2 Give out a copy of the worksheet to every student and ask them to look at **section A**. Refer to the instructions. Remind students that there is no one correct answer and they can make other suggestions. Divide the class into pairs/threes, start the activity and circulate. Have a brief whole-class discussion to review ideas at the end.

POSSIBLE ANSWERS
1 e + stop talking, look at them and wait for them to finish **2** d **3** c **4** a or b

3 Refer to the instructions for **section B** and develop a whole-class discussion.

POSSIBLE ANSWERS

1 Questions that seem to be a request for attention; hostile questions; if you need a few seconds thinking time

2 Difficult questions; open-ended questions of general interest; where you want audience participation; if you need a few seconds thinking time

3 Where one person in the audience is clearly the best person to answer

4 Refer to the instructions for **section C**. Divide the class into pairs, start the activity and circulate.

ANSWERS
1 Clarify **2** Redirect to the questioner **3** Redirect to the group **4** Redirect to another person **5** Control the timing.
(Give the students this tip: When you redirect, listen to the speaker and summarize their contribution on the board. When they finish use this summary to add your own comments.)

5 Refer to the instructions for **section D**. Set a time limit of four minutes for the presentation. Ask students to choose a topic and allow a few minutes for individual preparation. Emphasize that students should only write down two or three main points.

6 Just before the presentations, write on the board a phrase for finishing and asking for questions such as:
   – *Right, I'll finish there. Thank you very much for your attention. And now, if anyone has any questions, I'd be pleased to try to answer them.*
   Then refer to the audience questions in the box.

7 Ask students to give their presentations in turn, finishing by using the phrase on the board. To encourage questions at the end join in yourself, modelling phrases from the box. Make a note of good/bad language use.

8 Hold a short feedback slot.

7.4
Dealing with questions

A Match each 'problem person' with one or more techniques. What else could you do?

Problem Person
Somebody who ...
1 ... whispers during your talk.
2 ... interrupts with an irrelevant question.
3 ... challenges you on a factual point.
4 ... asks a difficult question at the end.

Techniques
a Redirect the question back to the questioner.
b Thank them and ask the group to comment.
c Say they might be right and you will check later.
d Say you'll deal with that point later.
e Ignore them.

B Think of a situation when you would use each technique below.

1 Redirect to the questioner
2 Redirect to the group
3 Redirect to another person

C Complete the table with the five techniques in the box.

> **Redirect to another person   Redirect to the questioner**
> **Redirect to the group   Clarify   Control the timing**

1 _____	Let me check I understand. Are you asking ...? Well, it all depends what you mean by ... . Could you be a little more specific?
2 _____	That's a very interesting question. Could I ask you what your own view is? You must have thought quite a lot about this. What do you think?
3 _____	Anyone like to comment on that? Has anyone else had a similar problem?
4 _____	That's a good question, but I'm afraid it's not really my field. Mr. Hamad, can you help me to answer that? Asif, I think you know more about this.
5 _____	OK, we only have a few minutes left. Is there one last question? I'm afraid that's all we have time for. Thank you all very much for your attention.

D Choose a topic from the list below. Alternatively, choose one of your own. Give a very short presentation. Invite and deal with questions at the end.

- A future political/social problem in my country.
- Business and the environment.
- Doing business with people from other cultures.
- Join the New Age Foundation! Give us 10% of your salary and find inner peace.
- Give me $100! I'll turn it into $200 and we'll split the profit.

> **Audience questions**
> What exactly did you mean when you were talking about ...
> I was interested in your comments about ... Could you say a little more about that?
> Could I just go back to the point you made about ... Well, in my experience ...

AIM

To practise a variety of rhetorical techniques: questions, repeating sounds, repeating words, repeating patterns of words, using opposites.

TIME

40–50 minutes

PREPARATION

Make one copy of the worksheet (two pages) for each student in the class.

PROCEDURE

1 Write up on the board the word *Persuasion* and elicit the meaning (the art of influencing or impressing people). Ask students if they can think of any special language techniques in the context of presentations. Prompt by asking them to think of an effective presentation that they can remember, or of a politician speaking.

2 Give out a copy of the worksheet to every student and ask them to look at **section A**. Refer to the instructions. Divide the class into pairs, start the activity and circulate. (If students notice the letters in brackets tell them to ignore these for the moment).

ANSWERS

1 Questions where you give the answer yourself
2 Repeating sounds   **3** Repeating a word/pattern of words   **4** Stop-and-start repetition   **5** Using opposite words/contrasting ideas

3 Refer to the instructions for **section B**. Divide the class into pairs, start the activity and circulate.

ANSWERS

(a) Repeating pattern of words (on time, every time)
(b) Repeating pattern of words (Are you looking ...?)
(c) Stop-and-start repetition   **(d)** Stop-and-start repetition   **(e)** Repeating sounds ('w')   **(f)** Repeating sounds ('b')   **(g)** Question where you give the answer yourself   **(h)** Repeating sounds ('t')

A The examples below show the speaker trying to persuade the audience. Fill in headings 1–5 with techniques from the box.

> **Using opposite words/contrasting ideas   Questions where you give the answer yourself**
> **Repeating a word/pattern of words   Repeating sounds   Stop-and-start repetition**

1 _____

How often do your customers say 'It's urgent – we need delivery tomorrow'? With the FastTrack Parcel Service we deliver on time, every time. (a)
Which airline was voted 'Best Business Carrier' by First Flight magazine? United Airways.
Are you looking for a company with a detailed knowledge of the local market? Are you looking for a business partner with a strong reputation? Well, look no more. (b)
So what's the problem? The problem is ... (c)
So what's the answer? The answer is ... (d)

2 _____

Happy and healthy, relaxed and refreshed. That's how you'll feel after visiting the Double Diamond Health Club.
Beat the rest – choose the best.
The Power of Progress.
Software for leisure and learning.

3 _____

Do you want to save money on international phone calls – again and again and again?
The world's getting smaller all the time. The world is waiting for you. (e)
Executive Books – the best book service for the busiest managers. (f)
Triple 'A' Car Recovery Club – call us whatever the time, we'll reach you wherever you are.

4 _____

Just take a moment to look at our results. Results that have made us a leading player in the financial services industry.
You know about American management skills. And the place to learn those skills is the BMA Management School.

5 _____

Do you want high safety at low cost?
Global reach with local support.
Should you e-mail or fax? Use your Intranet or the Internet? There are so many ways to connect: you need Webfast network solutions. (g)
We're making a difference for tomorrow, today. (h)

B The examples from section A with a letter at the end all use more than one technique. Can you identify the second technique? For example, (a) also uses technique 3, a repeating pattern of words (*on time, every time*).

4 Refer to the instructions for **section C**. Remind class that more than one technique may be used. Divide the class into pairs, start the activity and circulate.

ANSWERS

1 a, c, d (journey/destination) **2** a, c, d (Europe/town) **3** c, d **4** b **5** c **6** d **7** b (phones/future), c, d (past/future) **8** c, d **9** b **10** b (comes/Conference), c, d (our/your) **11** b (achieve/ambition), c **12** b **13** b, c **14** a **15** b, c, d (individuals/team) **16** b, c

5 Refer to the instructions for **section D**. Ask students to choose about half a dozen examples that they like. Then tell them to stand up, spread themselves out in the room, and practise reading aloud their chosen examples (individually, standing up). Circulate and help. As a round-up, ask students to sit down again and then ask each student to go to the front of the class and read out one or two of their chosen examples.

6 Tell students to think about using these techniques in future presentations on the course.

The extracts below are from advertisements in business magazines, but the techniques of persuasion are the same for presentations. Identify the technique(s) using a–d. The first one has been done for you.

    a Questions
    b Repeating sounds
    c Repeating a word/pattern of words
    d Using opposite words/contrasting ideas

  1 Where do you need to be? How will you get there? Does it matter? Yes, it matters. The journey is the destination. <u>Singapore Airlines</u>   *a, c and d.*

  2 Wouldn't it be amazing if sending a package across Europe could be as simple as sending it across town? <u>UPS</u>

  3 So easy to enjoy, so hard to forget. <u>Singapore Tourist Promotion Board</u>

  4 From Chips To Ships. <u>Hyundai</u>

  5 All that listening leads to understanding. And understanding is the first step to improvement. <u>Phillips</u>

  6 Where Luxury Comes As Standard. <u>Budget Car Rental</u>

  7 Wherever you are, whatever you're doing, you want to stay in touch. In touch with work, with friends or with loved ones. ... Thanks to our past we give you phones with a future. <u>Panasonic</u>

  8 Two companies. One team. No problem. <u>British Steel</u>

  9 Discover Bangladesh. And let your business boom! <u>Bangladesh Board of Investment</u>

10 When it comes to your Conference, our priorities are your priorities. <u>Monaco Promotion</u>

11 We have the will, a will shared by 56,000 men and women. ... We have the resources, with offices in 23 countries, on 4 continents. ... It is this will, it is these resources, that will help us achieve our ambition. <u>AXA</u>

12 Failure. Finances. Future. <u>Digital</u>

13 It has 32 valves. It develops 290 bhp. It's the finest 4.0 litre V8 production engine ever released. ... Don't dream it. Drive it. <u>Jaguar</u>

14 Where do you want to go today? <u>Microsoft</u>

15 Information passes freely, ideas are shared, individuals become a team. <u>Lotus</u>

16 We deliver to clients all over the world, where they want it, when they want it. <u>DHL</u>

D Choose some examples from section C and practise speaking them. Use your voice to give maximum impact, like in a presentation. Think about:

  • where to pause
  • which words to emphasize

7.6

Persuasion 2

AIM

To practise emphasizing and minimizing an idea as a presentation technique.

TIME

40–50 minutes

PREPARATION

Make one copy of the worksheet for each student in the class.

PROCEDURE

1 Write up on the board this sentence:
   - *Presenter: 'Our prices are more expensive, but the quality justifies the additional cost.'*

   Ask students how this sounds (it is clear, but could sound aggressive; the price sounds like it could be very expensive). Indicate with an arrow where the students might insert some extra words:
   - *Our prices are ↑ more expensive, but ↑ the quality justifies the ↑ additional cost.*

   Elicit some words that could go where the arrows are (see A2 on the worksheet).

2 Give out a copy of the worksheet to every student and ask them to look at **section A**. Ask different students to read out the five examples, *without* the words in brackets. Then ask the same students to read the same examples, *with* the words in brackets. Develop a brief class discussion about the effect of the words in the brackets.

POSSIBLE ANSWERS

   - Without the words in brackets the effect is too simple, direct and aggressive.
   - The words in brackets either emphasize a point (give it more importance) or minimize a point (give it less importance: because it really has less importance; because it is something negative; or for understatement).
   - The consistent use of the type of language in the brackets makes the argument sound more balanced and reasonable, as though the speaker has considered the points carefully.

3 Refer to the instructions for **section B**. Divide the class into pairs, start the activity and circulate.

POSSIBLE ANSWERS

   1 (We've had a very good year, in fact) we've had an excellent year.
   2 (There is some truth in that, but I feel that) you're exaggerating (a little).
   3 (Perhaps) we'll go (just a bit) over budget, but I'm (100%) certain that we'll get the job done.
   4 In relation to inflation, (I tend to think) the outlook is (quite) good.
   5 (Basically,) our economy is healthy (– very healthy).
   6 Next year we'll recruit (substantially) more graduates, and (what's more,) they'll come from the local markets where we operate.

4 Tell the students that they will now practise using their voice to emphasize and minimize. Tell them that they will say sentences A1–A5 and B1–B6 paying attention to the words in brackets. Write up on the board:
   Try:
   - *pausing just before the words in brackets*
   - *saying the words in brackets with a slightly higher voice*
   - *saying the words in brackets a little slower*

   Model some examples yourself with choral/individual repetition. Then divide the class into pairs and ask students to practise together. Start the activity and circulate. As a round-up, ask some students to read examples to the class.

5 Refer to the instructions for **section C** and the language summary in the box. Remind students that this would be a good chance to practise the techniques from worksheet 7.5 as well. Ask students to start preparing/writing their presentations individually in class and finish for homework. Note that the topic can be general as well as business. Circulate and help with vocabulary. In the next lesson the students give their presentations in turn, finishing by inviting questions. Make a note of good/bad language use.

6 Hold a short feedback slot.

7.6
Persuasion 2

A Say all the sentences below *without* the words in brackets.

1 (It seems to me that) four months is (a bit) optimistic.
2 Our prices are (relatively) more expensive, but (I think that) the quality justifies the (small) additional cost.
3 (Actually,) our reputation in the industry is (extremely) good.
4 (To some extent) our share price is (a little) overvalued, but I don't think it's a significant factor.
5 (Of course) every company has suffered from the recent recession, but (on the whole I feel) we have done (very) well to maintain our market share at 10%.

Now say the sentences again, this time *with* the words in brackets. What is the effect?

B Study the sentences below. First identify the main idea. Then put brackets round extra words and phrases that are just used to emphasize and minimize this main idea.

1 We've had a very good year, in fact we've had an excellent year.
2 There is some truth in that, but I feel that you're exaggerating a little.
3 Perhaps we'll go just a bit over budget, but I'm 100% certain that we'll get the job done.
4 In relation to inflation, I tend to think the outlook is quite good.
5 Basically, our economy is healthy – very healthy.
6 Next year we'll recruit substantially more graduates, and what's more, they'll come from the local markets where we operate.

C Write a short presentation on any subject you feel strongly about. Practise using a variety of techniques to persuade your audience that you are right.

Emphasizing a point (giving it more importance)

Emphasizing a point	*Actually, ... In fact, ... Basically, ... To put it simply, ...*
Adding a second point	*What's more, ... Besides (that), ... In addition (to that), ...*
Repeating more strongly	*It's fast. In fact, it's one of the fastest on the market*

Minimizing a point (giving it less importance)

Minimizing a point	*I think ... I feel ... I tend to think ... It seems to me that ...*
Using 'but' as a balance	*To some extent ..., but ... Perhaps ..., but on the whole ...*

Emphasizing/minimizing nouns

++ *a substantial* (investment) *a considerable* (risk) *a major* (decision)
+ *a significant* (factor) *an important* (opportunity)
- *a small* (mistake) *a slight* (difference of opinion) *a bit of a* (change)

Emphasizing/minimizing comparative adjectives

++ *substantially/considerably/much* (more expensive)
+ *significantly/relatively* (cheaper)
- *marginally/a little/slightly* (smaller)

AIM

To practise presenting a project: objectives, schedules, resources, budgets, progress.

TIME

40–50 minutes

PREPARATION

Make one copy of the worksheet for each student in the class.

PROCEDURE

1 Write up on the board the heading *Project management* and below this the words *schedule*, *budget* and *deadline*. Elicit the meanings (schedule = plan/timetable; budget = an amount of money given for a project; deadline = a date by which something must be done). Ask the students what other words will be useful when describing a project and brainstorm ideas to the board.

2 Give out a copy of the worksheet to every student and ask them to look at **section A**. Refer to the instructions. Divide the class into pairs, start the activity and circulate.

ANSWERS

1 stage, step, phase 2 objective, aim, target, goal ('objective'/'aim' are often more general, 'target'/'goal' are often more specific and quantifiable) 3 choice, option, alternative 4 schedule, plan 5 task, job 6 deadline, time limit

3 Refer to the instructions for **section B**. Divide the class into pairs, start the activity and circulate.

ANSWERS

1 c 2 e 3 a 4 b 5 h 6 i 7 j 8 f 9 g
10 d

4 Refer to the instructions for **section C**. Divide the class into pairs, start the activity and circulate.

ANSWERS

1 set 2 objectives 3 meet 4 requirements
5 carried out 6 tests 7 meet 8 deadline 9 be
10 over budget 11 on schedule 12 reach
13 target 14 make up lost time

5 Refer to the instructions for **section D** and the four points that help give a structure to the presentation. Ask students to start preparing/writing their presentations individually in class and finish for homework. Circulate and help with vocabulary. In the next lesson the students give their presentations in turn, finishing with questions from the audience. Make a note of good/bad language use.

6 Hold a short feedback slot.

7.7
Presenting a project

Worksheet

A Which of these words have a similar meaning? Put them into 6 groups.

stage objective choice schedule step aim option task
target plan deadline alternative job goal phase time limit

B Match the verbs on the left with the words/phrases on the right.

1	to meet (= satisfy)	**a**	tests
2	to meet (= satisfy)	**b**	problems
3	to carry out (= do)	**c**	a deadline
4	to solve	**d**	lost time
5	to increase	**e**	the customer's requirements
6	to reach	**f**	behind schedule / on schedule / ahead of schedule
7	to set (= define)	**g**	under budget / within budget / over budget
8	to be	**h**	costs
9	to be	**i**	a target
10	to make up (= recover)	**j**	clear objectives

C Use words from section B to complete this presentation extract about the schedule for manufacturing an industrial component. You will have to change the tense of one verb.

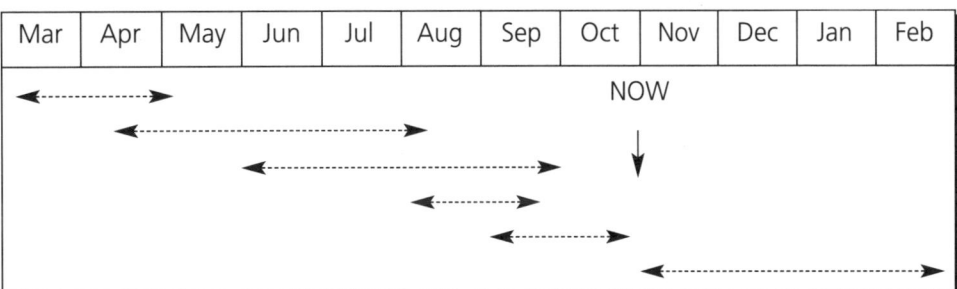

Project Step	Mar	Apr	May	Jun	Jul	Aug	Sep	Oct	Nov	Dec	Jan	Feb
First design									NOW			
Build and test												
Final design												
Order materials												
Prepare machines												
Production												

Before we started on the design, it was necessary to (1) _____ clear (2) _____ so that we could be sure to (3) _____ all our customers' (4) _____ . After building the prototype in May we then (5) _____ _____ extensive (6) _____ . We wanted to finalize the design by the end of September, and we managed to (7) _____ this (8) _____ . However, some of the raw materials that we need for production are now more expensive, and so it looks like the final cost is going to (9) _____ a little (10) _____ _____ . As regards timing, we have finished preparing the machines and so the project is (11) _____ _____ . I'm sure we can (12) _____ our production (13) _____ of 50 units per week from January onwards. If we have to (14) _____ _____ _____ _____ we can run the machines at night for a short period, although that would increase costs.

D Prepare and give a presentation on a project that you are currently involved with. You may want to draw a planning schedule on the board before you begin (like in section C).

1 Description of and schedule for the project
2 Resources: a) materials b) human resources
3 Budget
4 Progress: Is the project on schedule? Is the project within budget?
              What are the problems? How are you solving them?

► **PHOTOCOPIABLE**

7.8

Presenting a process/system

AIM

To practise presenting a process or system: describing the stages/parts, referring to sequence, using the passive voice.

TIME

40–50 minutes

PREPARATION

Make one copy of the worksheet for each student in the class.

(Option) The suggested lead-in at stage 1 below is a live listening where you model the target language yourself. You may wish to prepare this by: making notes; sketching a diagram or flow chart for copying onto the board; recording the description onto cassette.

PROCEDURE

1 Write up on the board *Describing a process/system*. Tell the students that you are going to describe a process, and that you want them to listen carefully and note down any special language you use. Then describe a process (e.g. how you prepare your lessons, the enrolment procedure at your school etc.), modeling the target language from the worksheet. At the end ask the students what language they noticed.

2 Give out a copy of the worksheet to every student and ask them to look at **section A**. Refer to the first line of instructions and the table. Ask the students if they can see any phrases from your lead-in. Then refer to the instructions for the task. Divide the class into pairs, start the activity and circulate.

ANSWERS (BY PARAGRAPH)

The process ... involves / can be divided into four or five main stages
First / When the supplier receives
Next / The l.c. is sent / as soon as it arrives / After that / the goods are shipped
The next step involves / Having done this / When they arrive / payment is released / the money is transferred / first / and then / while
Finally / The whole process is used for making sure

3 Discuss with the class the mixture of active and passive in the example text. Ask what the balance is (there is more use of the active). Ask what the problem is if you use the passive too much (it sounds very formal and can be difficult to understand). Elicit and write on the board when the passive is used:
Using the passive: when you want to direct attention to the process/action, not the person doing it (the person may be unknown or unimportant)

4 Refer to the instructions for **section B**. Ask students to start preparing/writing their presentations individually in class and finish for homework. Circulate and help with vocabulary. In the next lesson the students give their presentations in turn, finishing with questions from the audience. Make a note of good/bad language use.

5 Hold a short feedback slot.

7.8
Presenting a process/system

Worksheet

A The language in the table is useful for describing processes and systems.

Division into parts	X includes/involves ... X is composed of/consists of ... X can be divided into three main stages/steps/parts/types
Sequence	First, ... First of all, ... At the first stage we ... Second, ... The second step involves ... Then, ... Next, ... After that, ... Following that, ... At the next stage we ... Finally, ... The final step is to ... At the final stage we ...
Time reference	**earlier:** Before that, ... **during the same period:** Meanwhile, ..., while ... **immediately after:** When ... As soon as ... **later:** After (+ *ing* form of verb) Having (+ p.p. of verb)
Passive voice	The food is sorted/prepared/cooked/checked for quality/measured/put into cans/labeled/dispatched This machine is used to (+ infinitive) / is used for (+ *ing* form of verb)

The text below explains how a customer in Angola pays for some agricultural machinery from a supplier in Brazil. Underline all the examples of language from the table.

The process of paying for goods involves banks in Angola, Brazil and New York and can be divided into four or five main stages.

First, the customer in Angola contacts the local agent of an AAA-rated New York bank. The customer deposits some funds or gives a guarantee to cover payment of the goods. This allows him/her to place the order with the supplier in Brazil. When the supplier receives the order, he/she issues a 'pro-forma' invoice (an invoice sent in advance of goods) and sends it to the customer.

Next, the customer in Angola takes the pro-forma invoice to the local bank. The bank issues a letter of credit (l.c.) – this means that the order cannot be cancelled. The l.c. is sent to a Brazilian agent of the same New York bank, and as soon as it arrives the agent contacts the supplier. After that the supplier can process the order and the goods are shipped.

The next step involves the Brazilian agent checking all the documents to see if everything is correct. Having done this, the agent sends the documents to the main bank in New York. The New York bank checks everything one more time and sends the documents to the agent in Angola. When they arrive, the customer's payment is released and the money is transferred, first to New York and then to Brazil. This usually happens while the goods are still in transit.

Finally, the supplier receives the money. The whole process is used for making sure there are no problems with payment.

B Prepare and give a presentation on a process or system that is important in your work. You may want to draw a diagram or list the main stages on the board before you begin.

7.9a

Describing trends 1

WORKSHEETS 7.9 TO 7.11

Worksheets 7.9, 7.10 and 7.11 provide language work and skills practice for the language of trends and should be followed in sequence. If you only have time for two activities, use 7.9 and 7.11. If you only have time for one activity, use 7.11 because of the opportunity for personalization at the end.

AIM

To practise a variety of language for describing trends: verbs and nouns referring to movement of a graph, qualifying adverbs and adjectives, linking words.

TIME

50–60 minutes

PREPARATION

Make one copy of the worksheet (two pages) for each student in the class.

PROCEDURE

1 Write up on the board the heading *Trends*. Elicit the meaning of 'trend' (a general tendency or change in direction). Draw on the board three arrows: upward, horizontal and downward. Under each one write *Last year sales ...* . Then elicit one or two verbs to complete each sentence (e.g. went up/increased; stayed the same/remained constant; went down/decreased). Draw one or two other upward arrows with different gradients and elicit some adverbs (e.g. 'Sales increased a little/considerably').

2 Give out a copy of the worksheet to every student and ask them to look at **section A**. Refer to the instructions. Divide the class into pairs, start the activity and circulate.

ANSWERS

1 c 2 a 3 b 4 e 5 f 6 d 7 a, b, d, e 8 c, f
9 a, e 10 b, c, d, f 11 a, d, f 12 b, c, e

3 Refer to the instructions for **section B**. Divide the class into pairs, start the activity and circulate.

ANSWERS

Verbs: go up/improve/rise/increase; be stable/stay the same/remain constant; go down/fall/decrease
Nouns: growth/improvement/rise/increase; no change; collapse/fall/decrease
Linking words: because/because of/due to ('due to' is followed by a noun phrase); but/although ('but' makes a contrast between two clauses of equal importance; 'although' introduces a clause which is less important and surprising after the first clause); In relation to/As regards
Bullet point: went up, grew, rose, fell

4 Refer to the instructions for **section C**. Remind the class that they saw examples of the two types of structure in section A. Divide the class into pairs, start the activity and circulate.

ANSWERS

2 We had a sharp rise in profits. 3 We saw a significant fall in unemployment. 4 There was no change in house prices.

7.9a
Describing trends 1

A Match these adverbs with their definitions:

Speed
1	quickly	**a**	a slow, step-by-step change
2	gradually	**b**	a constant, regular change
3	steadily	**c**	a rapid change

Amount
4	significantly	**d**	a small change
5	sharply	**e**	a large change
6	slightly	**f**	a sudden change

Now study phrases a–f and answer questions 7–12.

a Sales grew slowly.
b We saw a steady improvement in our brand image.
c We had a considerable decrease in our market share.
d Our profits rose sharply.
e There was a slight growth in inflation.
f Unemployment fell significantly.

Which of the phrases a–f:

7 describe a movement up?
8 describe a movement down?
9 describe a small movement?
10 describe a medium or large movement?
11 have a 'verb + adverb' structure?
12 have an 'adjective + noun' structure?

B Complete the table with words from the box. Some words are used twice.

> improve improvement fall (x2) although rise (x2) increase (x2)
> stay the same As regards decrease (x2) due to remain constant

	▲	►	▼
Verbs	go up	be stable	go down
Nouns	growth	no change	collapse

	cause	contrast	moving to a new topic
Linking words	*because* (+ subject + verb) *because of* (+ noun phrase)	*but*	*In relation to*

• Write the past simple of these verbs:

go up _____ grow _____ rise _____ fall _____

C Rewrite these 'verb + adverb' phrases as 'adjective + noun' phrases.

1 Sales grew slowly. ► There was a _slow growth in sales._

2 Profits rose sharply. ► We had a _____

3 Unemployment fell significantly. ► We saw a _____

4 House prices were stable. ► There was _____

► **PHOTOCOPIABLE**

5 Refer to the instructions and example graphs and notes for **section D**. Circulate and help with vocabulary. When they finish, one or two students can give their presentations, finishing with questions from the audience. Make a note of good/bad language use.

6 Hold a short feedback slot.

7 Refer to the instructions and role notes for **section E**. Encourage students to try this as fluency practice without preparation, but weaker groups may need a few minutes to make notes first for their turn as Student A. Divide the class into pairs and appoint As and Bs. Remind students to change roles and repeat when they finish. Set a time limit of 5 minutes for each person. Start the activity, circulate and make a note of good/bad language use.

8 Hold a short feedback slot.

D Choose two trends in your life related to the theme of 'time management'. For example:

Time spent ... with children / with friends / in the garden / doing sport / learning English
doing homework / abroad / in meetings / writing reports / doing overtime

Prepare simple graphs and write notes to practise the language of trends. The examples below will give you some ideas. Notice the use of language from section B.

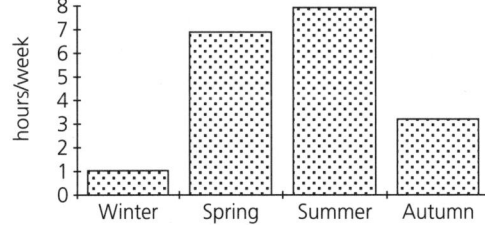

Time spent in the garden last year

– Vertical axis shows hours per week, horizontal axis shows seasons
– Little time spent in the garden in winter due to cold weather
– More time in spring, although mainly at weekends
– Time rose in summer because of holidays and meals outside
– Steady decrease during autumn

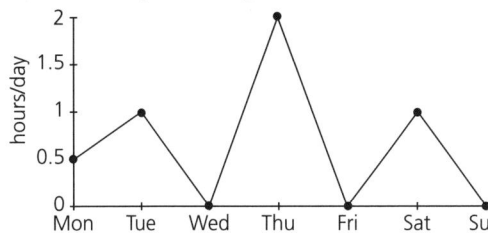

Time spent doing homework last week

– Vertical axis shows hours per day, horizontal axis shows days
– Little time on Monday because of feeling tired
– Small increase on Tuesday (I read a magazine article)
– Fall to zero on Wednesday, but dramatic rise on Thursday due to time preparing presentation
– As regards the weekend, only one hour on Saturday

E Work with a partner. Change roles when you finish.

Student A   Describe some trends
• in your company last year (sales, profits, market share etc.)
• in your country last year (inflation, unemployment, house prices etc.).

Examples: *Last year our profits fell slightly, due to difficult market conditions.*
In relation to house prices, there was a small increase, although it was about the same as inflation.

Student B   Ask Student A to explain the trends in a little more detail.

Can you tell me a little more about that?
So why ... ?
And what is the Government doing about that?

7.10a
Describing trends 2

AIM

To review and extend language for describing trends:
saying numbers, choosing appropriate verb tenses,
linking words, transitive and intransitive verbs.

TIME

50–60 minutes

PREPARATION

Make one copy of the worksheet (two pages) for each
student in the class.

PROCEDURE

1 Write up on the board eight figures: *670; 6,700;
67,000; 60,700; 600,000; 670,000; 6,700,000; 6.7
million*. Elicit how to say them and write up any
that the students find difficult (six hundred and
seventy; six thousand seven hundred; sixty seven
thousand; sixty thousand seven hundred; six
hundred thousand; six hundred and seventy
thousand; six million seven hundred thousand; six
point seven million). Note that in the
American/British system a comma is used to mark
off thousands, and a full stop represents a decimal
point. In many Latin countries exactly the opposite
is the case. Other problem areas are likely to be:
 – remembering to pause where there is a comma to
 make the number easier to say and understand
 (there is no pause if it is a round number with
 only zeros after the comma)
 – the position of 'and' (which in British English
 goes between the hundreds and tens)
 – the fact that hundred, thousand, etc., do not have
 an 's' (they only do in phrases like 'hundreds of
 people').

2 Give out a copy of the worksheet to every student
and ask them to look at **section A**. Refer to the
instructions. In open class ask students to read out
the figures round the circle. Go back frequently to
problem areas and check again with different
students randomly round the group. Monitor
especially for the problem areas above.

ANSWERS (SELECTED)

14/40 – four<u>teen</u>/<u>forty</u> (different word stress when
said in isolation, same – first syllable – when said in
a sentence)
2,500 – two thousand, five hundred/twenty-five
hundred
25,600 – twenty-five thousand, six hundred (no *and*)
25,660 – twenty-five thousand, six hundred and sixty
340,000 – three hundred and forty thousand
3,400,000 – three million, four hundred thousand
3.8 – three point eight
3.88 – three point eight eight (not eighty-eight)

3 Refer to the instructions and graphs for **section B**.
Explain to the students that they will have a chance
to talk about their own company in a later lesson (in
fact worksheet 7.11). Say that here they will
practise language from worksheet 7.9, and also verb
tenses. Refer to the 'Sales' and 'Contribution of two
best selling products' graphs and elicit the various
tenses that will be used. For each tense write an
example on the board:
 – *<u>Last year</u> sales <u>increased</u> in December (past
 simple for last year)*
 – *<u>This year</u> the first quarter <u>has been</u> a little better
 than the same period last year (present perfect
 for this year up to now)*
 – *<u>At the moment</u> Product B <u>is making</u> an important
 contribution to our profits (present continuous
 for activity in progress at the moment)*
 – *I think sales <u>will probably/probably won't reach</u>
 £25 million <u>by the end of the year</u> (the 'will'
 future for predictions)*

4 Refer to the instructions under the graphs. Divide
the class into pairs. If possible, put together
students with a similar business background. Allow
10 minutes for the pairs to invent their company
name and business, study and discuss the graphs,
and fill in the information in the final box. It is
likely that the imaginary company will be similar to
one or both of the students' real companies.
Encourage them to use their real-life experience to
explain the movements up and down, give real
identities to Product A and B etc.

5 Refer to the instructions for **section C**. Divide the
class into new pairs. Appoint As and Bs and remind
the students to change roles when they finish. Set a
time limit of 5 minutes for each person. Start the
activity, circulate and make a note of good/bad
language use.

6 Hold a short feedback slot.

A Make sure that you can say numbers correctly. Say these.

14   40   17   70
2,500 (two ways)   2,560   2,516   25,600   25,660
200,000   225,800   340,000   3,400,000
3.8   3.88

B Study the graphs below which show information for an imaginary company. Note that it is now April and the graphs refer to last year and the first quarter of this year.

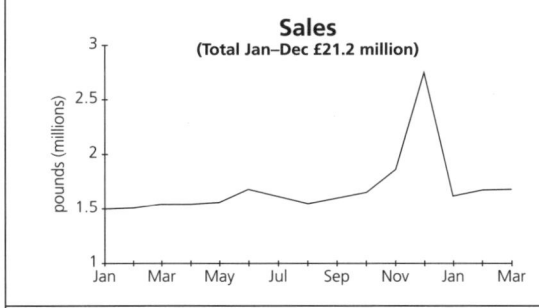

Sales
(Total Jan–Dec £21.2 million)

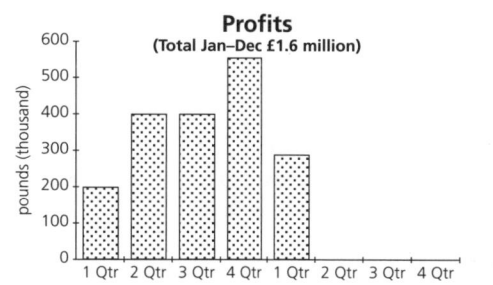

Profits
(Total Jan–Dec £1.6 million)

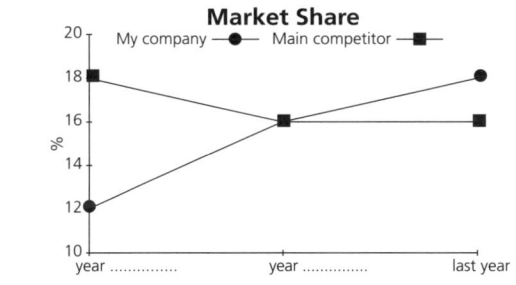

Market Share
My company ●   Main competitor ■

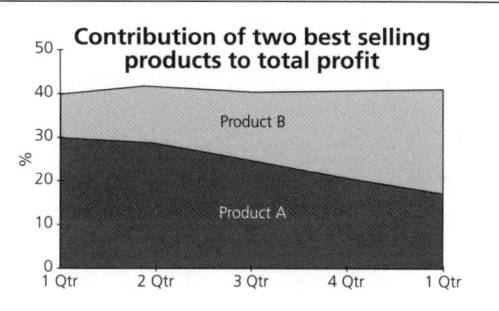

Contribution of two best selling products to total profit

Product B
Product A

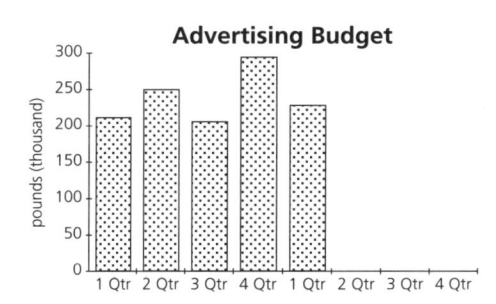

Advertising Budget

Market predictions for this current year, based on the figures above:

Total sales   _____

Total profits   _____

Market share   _____

Ideas for new products:

_____

Now work with a partner. You both work for the imaginary company referred to in the graphs.

Name of company: _____

Main business area: _____

The graphs refer to your company, so:
• Describe and discuss the trends
• Invent reasons for the main movements during your discussion
• Complete the market predictions and think of ideas for new products

C Now work with a new partner. Student A discuss the business you have just invented: describe and explain the graphs and talk about your predictions for the current year. Student B ask questions. Change roles when you finish.

7 Refer to the instructions for **section D**. Divide the class into pairs, start the activity and circulate. Check the answers to 1–6 and the information in the grammar box before referring to the bullet point. (Grammar box: the three conjunctions for contrast are not interchangeable and the box explains their usage in simple terms. If you read out the completed examples 4–6 as you refer to the usage notes, students should feel the difference and more explanation will be unnecessary. In fact the differences are as follows: 'although' introduces a subordinate clause which is surprising; 'in spite of' introduces a subordinate clause that makes the main clause seem surprising; 'whereas' introduces a contrasting clause but it is not really subordinate or surprising and so is more like 'but'. The element of surprise with 'although' and 'in spite of' might also be due to their sentence position, the surprising clause coming at the end.)

ANSWERS

1 because of/due to   **2** because   **3** led to/resulted in
4 although   **5** In spite of   **6** whereas
Bullet point: 'in spite of' is followed by a noun clause; 'although' and 'whereas' are followed by subject + verb
(For higher level groups finish section D by writing up on the board *while*, *even though* and *despite* and asking which words they are the same as.)

8 Refer to the first line of instructions for **section E**. Ask one student to say all four phrases aloud and elicit from the group which is the incorrect phrase and why (the final phrase is impossible: the verb 'fall' is intransitive and cannot be used with an object). Refer to the task, divide the class into pairs, start the activity and circulate.

ANSWERS

1 increase/decrease   **2** cut/maintain   **3** grow/go down

9 (Homework) Refer to the instructions for **section F**. Ask students to write their presentations for homework. Correct the homework and hand it back as usual, but it is not necessary for students to actually give these presentations in class as they will all be quite similar to each other and to the activity in section B.

10 (Option) Leave one of the student's homework texts uncorrected (explain to the student why), and photocopy one copy of this for each student. In the next lesson ask students to try to correct/improve this text in pairs. In feedback listen to all the suggestions for reformulations and discuss with the class which is the best. Build up the reformulated text (or parts) on the board sentence by sentence.

7.10b
Describing trends 2

D Fill in the gaps using words from the box.

because	because of	led to	although	in spite of	due to	resulted in	whereas

Cause and result

1 Profits increased last month _____ / _____ our new sales campaign.

2 Profits increased last month _____ we had a new sales campaign.

3 Our new sales campaign _____ / _____ an increase in profits last month.

Contrast

4 We had a reasonable year in Asia, _____ sales fell a little in Japan.

5 _____ the fall in sales in Japan, we did quite well in the rest of Asia.

6 Sales in Asia last year were quite strong, _____ the previous year had been very disappointing.

---

although / in spite of / whereas

Although   In example 4 above the main information is about Asia. The other fact introduced by *although* (about Japan) contrasts with it and is surprising.

In spite of   In example 5 the main information is also about Asia. Now it is this that seems surprising.

Whereas   In example 6 there is a comparison of information of equal importance and no surprise.

- Look back at examples 4–6 and make grammar rules by crossing out the wrong words:

  although / in spite of / whereas is followed by a noun clause (no verb).
  although / in spite of / whereas are followed by subject + verb.

E One of these phrases sounds strange. Which one? What is the problem?

Prices increased   We increased our prices   Prices fell   We fell our prices

Read the information about 'Types of verb' and complete the examples with words from the box.

grow	increase	cut	go down	decrease	maintain

Types of verb

1 <u>Transitive/Intransitive verbs</u> can be used with or without an object.
We'll improve/recover/ _____ / _____ our market share.
And, using the same verbs:
Our market share will improve/recover/ _____ / _____ .

2 <u>Transitive verbs</u> are always followed by an object.
We'll raise/lower/ _____ / _____ her salary.
(*But not* Her salary will raise.)

3 <u>Intransitive verbs</u> are never followed by an object.
Inflation will rise/fall/ _____ / _____ .
(*But not* This policy will rise inflation.)

F Refer back to section B. This time prepare a written presentation on trends in your imaginary company. Use a good variety of language for describing and explaining trends.

▶

PHOTOCOPIABLE

7.11a

Company trends

AIM

To review and extend language for describing trends and personalize this for the students' own companies.

TIME

50–60 minutes

PREPARATION

Make one copy of the worksheet (two pages) for each student in the class.

PROCEDURE

1 Write up on the board *Company trends*. Tell students that they are going to revise the language of trends and then prepare a presentation of trends in their own companies. Re-elicit some of the language from worksheets 7.9 and 7.10. (If you have not done these you will have to pre-teach some of the key language as an extended lead–in, e.g. draw an imaginary sales graph with movements up and down on the board and elicit and write up a description and explanation of the main movements. Include a variety of verbs and adverbs, linking words and tenses).

2 Give out a copy of the worksheet to every student and ask them to look at **section A**. Refer to the instructions. Divide the class into pairs, start the activity and circulate.

ANSWERS

1 to stay the same   2 to increase   3 to fall
4 to be above/below   5 to reach a peak
6 to drop back   7 to hit a low   8 to recover
9 to fluctuate and then to level off
10 to remain high   11 to stand at

3 Refer to the instructions for **section B**. Divide the class into pairs, start the activity and circulate.

ANSWERS

1 pie chart   2 bar chart   3 table   4 (line) graph
5 graph   6 half   7 units   8 to   9 figure (5.8m is a number, but when a number refers to something specific we say 'a figure/value of 5.8m')   10 by
11a by   11b of   11c in   12a good news
12b bad news   12c good news   12d good news
('to improve' = 'to get better' and the opposite is 'to deteriorate' = 'to get worse')

7.11a
Company trends

Worksheet

A Label these graphs with words from the box.

> to increase   to fall   to stay the same   to be above/below   to reach a peak   to hit a low
> to drop back   to recover   to stand at   to remain high   to fluctuate and then to level off

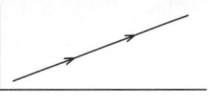

1 _____

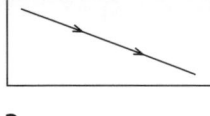

2 _____

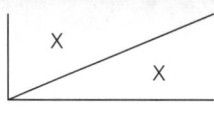

3 _____

4 _____

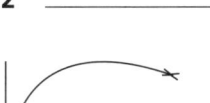

5 _____

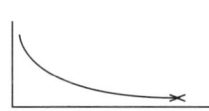

6 _____

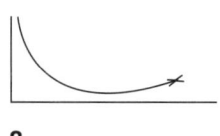

7 _____

8 _____

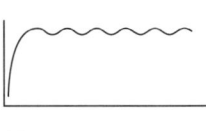

9 _____

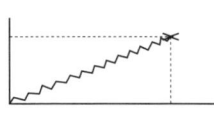

10 _____

11 _____

B Answer questions 1–12.

Label these charts with words from the box.

> (line) graph   bar chart   pie chart   table

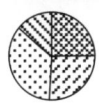

1 _____

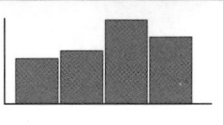

2 _____

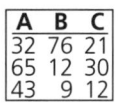

3 _____

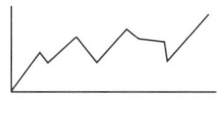

4 _____

Choose the correct words to complete this presentation extract.

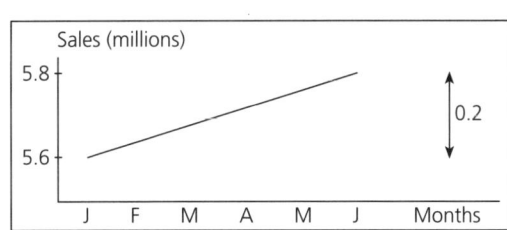

I'd like you to look at the (5) *graph/graphic*, which shows our sales in the first (6) *half/quarter* of this year. The vertical axis represents sales in millions of (7) *unities/units*. As you can see from the graph, sales rose from 5.6m in January (8) *until/to* a (9) *figure/number* of 5.8m in June. In other words, sales rose (10) *with/by* 0.2m.

11 Choose the correct preposition.

  a Sales increased *by/of/in* 3%.   (after a verb)

  b There was an increase in sales *by/of/in* 3%. (after a noun and before an amount)

  c There was a 3% increase *by/of/in* sales.   (after a noun and before the topic)

12 Say if these things are good news or bad news:

  a Sales increased. **b** Inflation increased. **c** Sales improved. **d** Inflation improved.

4 Refer to the instructions for **section C**. Divide the class into pairs, start the activity and circulate.

ANSWERS

1 figures **2** beginning **3** recover **4** considerable improvement **5** levelled **6** reach **7** stable **8** spite **9** rising steadily **10** relation **11** due **12** over

Notice that the text models a lot of the language of trends in context, particularly a good variety of verb tenses. You may wish to elicit reasons for the choice of verb tense each time as revision and preparation for section D.

5 Refer to the instructions for **section D**. Divide students into pairs. Ask them to cover the text in section C with a piece of paper, but leave the four graphs showing. Elicit and write up some questions for the Bs:

– *Can you tell me a little more about that?*
– *So why ...?*

Appoint As and Bs. The As talk about the graphs, inventing reasons (it is not a memory test). The Bs ask questions. They change roles and repeat when they finish. Start the activity, circulate and make a note of good/bad language use.

6 Hold a short feedback slot.

7 Refer to the instructions for **section E**. Prompt students to think of the kinds of graphs, charts and trends they have to talk about in their real jobs. Ask students to start preparing their presentations individually in class and finish for homework. Circulate and help with vocabulary. In the next lesson the students give their presentations in turn, finishing with questions from the audience. Make a note of good/bad language use.

8 Hold a short feedback slot.

7.11b
Company trends

C This extract is from a presentation about company results. The presenter is talking about the four graphs below. Fill in the gaps using words from the box.

spite	improvement	figures	considerable	leveled	recover
reach	due	beginning	rising	over	stable	steadily	relation

Earlier this year our sales (1) _____ were not looking good. Sales had fallen to 1100 units, and at the (2) _____ of March we appointed a new Marketing Director. During April sales began to (3) _____ , although they fell back again in May, probably as a result of seasonal factors. In July and August there was a (4) _____ _____ , but in the last few months the growth in sales has (5) _____ off and we probably won't (6) _____ our target of 1600 units by the end of the year.

Our market share remains (7) _____ at about 12% in (8) _____ of very aggressive discounting by our main competitor.

Income from company investments is (9) _____ _____ at the moment, while our income from sales has, unfortunately, been rather flat over recent years.

In (10) _____ to the economic context in which we operate, the outlook remains uncertain. This is largely (11) _____ to changes in interest rates, which have been going up gradually (12) _____ the last few months.

Sales this year (units)

Market share (%)

Income (million dollars)

Interest rates (%)

D Cover the presentation extract above with a piece of paper but leave the graphs showing. Work with a partner. Student A describe and explain the graphs in your own words. Student B ask questions.

E Prepare and give a presentation to describe and explain some trends in your company. Use simple graphs to support your presentation. Invite and answer questions at the end.

AIM

To provide a stimulus for choosing a personalized presentation topic.

TIME

variable

PREPARATION

Make one copy of the worksheet for each student in the class.

Consider making one copy of the 'Cue-Cards' advice box below for each student. See stage 2 below.

Make arrangements to use audio or video recording facilities for the day of the presentations. See stage 4 below.

PROCEDURE

1 Give out a copy of the worksheet to every student some days before you want them to give their first main presentation in class. Set a time limit for the presentation (e.g. 15 minutes). Ask the students to start thinking about which topic they will choose and then to prepare the presentation. Remind the students to use any language and techniques they have learnt earlier in this module.

2 (Option) Give out and discuss the notes on 'cue-cards' below. (A 'cue' is a signal for someone to speak in a play).

3 On the day of the presentations, allocate reasonable time for each presentation as students invariably go over time and there will be questions. At the end of each presentation ask a first question yourself if necessary to get the ball rolling. Consider writing individual feedback sheets during the presentation.

4 (Option) On the day consider also:
   - calling in students from another class (or a stand-by teacher) to act as an audience
   - recording the presentation onto video tape for the student to review their performance and perhaps comment on their own presentation skills
   - recording the presentation onto audio tape for later correction and reformulation (this is a must for one-to-one students).

CUE-CARDS

To read or not to read? That is the question. The problem with reading your presentation is that you will be looking down most of the time. You will be unable to see audience reactions; your voice will be monotonous; your own natural enthusiasm for the subject will be hidden; your body language will be poor. But preparing the text in full can be useful for a learner of English and gives you some security. So here is one possible solution.

1 Write the full text. Work on vocabulary and grammar.

2 Practise reading parts of the text aloud. Work on pausing, emphasizing key ideas, intonation and pronunciation. Aim for maximum impact. Consider recording this onto audio tape. Keep the tape – listen to it in your car!

3 Summarize the main points and write them on a series of postcards. These are your 'cue-cards'. Cue-cards fit into your pocket, won't distract an audience, and are easy to correct or replace. When preparing your cue-cards remember to:
   - number the cards and put them in order
   - use different colours
   - write quotes, statistics and sources in full, but use key words for everything else
   - include reminders for when to refer to your visual aids
   - include occasional 'performance' messages to yourself, like: Slow down! Look round the audience! Smile and take a deep breath! Speak louder!

4 Practise giving your presentation with the cue-cards. Work on your presentation skills.

7.12
Presentation topics

My company/products
- Introduction to my company: history, structure (organigram), main products, main markets
- Product/service range of my company; or description and features of one specific product/service.
- Detailed physical description of one of my products:
  - Dimensions (length, width/depth, height, weight, volume/capacity)
  - Shape and colour (rectangular, circular, L-shaped, curved, cylindrical, in the shape of a ...)
  - Materials (plastic, steel, cotton, polyester, wood, polystyrene, leather, metal)
  - Technical specifications (speed, electricity consumption, pieces per minute)
  - Features (high-quality, advanced design, economical, easy to use, reliable, efficient)
- SWOT analysis of my company (strengths, weaknesses, opportunities and threats)
- STEP analysis of my market (external factors that affect the business environment: sociological, technological, economic and political)
- Figures and trends: sales by value (income) / sales by volume (units sold) / sales figures for one particular product / profits / market share / advertising budget / other budgets / number of employees / expansion plans etc.
- Market trends in my area of business
- The impact of new technology on my business
- Annual Report. Include in one presentation:
  1 Profit and loss account / Balance sheet / Cash flow
  2 Economic forecast for my country next year
  3 Forecast of costs
  4 Brief SWOT analysis (strengths, weaknesses, opportunities and threats)
  5 Business objectives for next year
  6 Market predictions for next year: sales, profits, market share, new products, product mix
  7 People, motivation and training
  8 Main strategic issues
- Company Philosophy. For example:
  - 'Selling solutions not products'
  - 'Excellence in customer service'
  - 'Thinking globally, acting locally'
  - 'Quality: more than just a certificate'
  - 'Corporate responsibility: community and environment'
  - ? (your own)

My job/profession
- Recent developments in my professional area
- My main functions and responsibilities

My country/city
- Trends in economic and financial indicators – past, present and future – such as: inflation, unemployment, interest rates, earnings (wages), consumer spending (retail sales), GDP (gross domestic product), public spending, currency/dollar, imports, exports, house prices etc.
- Brief introduction to my country: population and geography, political and social situation, main industries and services, SWOT analysis of the economy
- A social or environmental issue that is currently in the news
- A new infrastructure project in my country/city that is being planned/built

Authentic text
- Summary of an interesting newspaper/magazine article, finishing with a personal opinion and questions for the group to discuss

7.13

Mini-presentation

WORKSHEET 7.13

This worksheet is a framework for any short presentation where you want to encourage fluency rather than detailed language work or reading word for word. Students can use it several times for different presentations. It would be appropriate for distribution before preparing a presentation for homework.

AIM

To provide a framework for writing short notes as preparation for a presentation.

TIME

variable

PREPARATION

Make one copy of the worksheet for each student in the class.

PROCEDURE

1 Give out a copy of the worksheet to every student. Refer to the main headings and remind students how they describe the basic structure of a presentation. Give the students time to read the phrases and clarify any doubts. Refer to the two groups of phrases in the middle of 'Main presentation' and elicit why they have been grouped (the first group are for referring to visual aids, the second group are signpost phrases). Similarly, refer to the grouping in 'Dealing with questions' (they are all for redirecting the question).

2 Explain to the students that they should just make brief notes as preparation. In the presentation itself they will develop the ideas as they speak.

Introduction

Can everyone see? Well, good morning ladies and gentleman. Thank you for coming.

Before we start I'd like to introduce myself. My name is ... and I am the ... (position) of ... (company).

I'm here today to talk about ...

I'm going to look at three main areas.

First, I'll talk about ...

After that I will ...

And finally ...

My presentation will take around 10 minutes. If you have any questions, I'll be happy to answer them at the end of my talk.

Main presentation

First of all, I'd like to look at ...

Any questions so far?

Secondly, ...

I must emphasize that ...

The question is ...

{ I'd like you to look at ... You will see that ...
As you can see from the graph, ...
The figures show that ...

{ If I can just side-track for a moment, ...
As I mentioned earlier, ...
I'll come back to that in a moment.
Now let's move on to the question of ...

This brings me to my last point, which is ...

As you know, ...

In general, ...

On the other hand ...

Finally, ...

Conclusion

In conclusion, let me briefly go through the main points again. First I talked about ..., then I described ..., and finally I ... .

Right, I think that's everything. Let me finish by thanking you very much for your attention. And now, if you have any questions, I'll be happy to try to answer them.

Dealing with questions

Could you be a little more specific? / Can I just check what you're asking?

{ You've raised an important point there. Could I ask what your own view is?
Anyone like to comment on that?
Jane, this is your area. Would you like to make a comment?

We only have a few minutes left. Is there one last question?

▶ **PHOTOCOPIABLE**

8.1

Your company and job

Teacher's Notes

WORKSHEET 8.1

This worksheet is very appropriate for *Day one, Lesson one*. The optional stages below reflect this and include a 'getting to know you' start to the lesson and a procedure for using the Needs Analysis at the end.

Allow a full morning for all the stages. The Needs Analysis is left until after doing the worksheet in order to give the students a chance to establish their identity in the group as early as possible.

AIM

To practise describing and discussing the students' own companies and jobs.

TIME

50–60 minutes (without the optional stages)

PREPARATION

Make one copy of the worksheet for each student in the class.
(Option) Make one copy of the Needs Analysis at the front of this Resource Pack. See stage 8 below.

PROCEDURE

1 (Option) Welcome everyone to the course. Divide the class into closed pairs. Ask the students to find out about their partner: name, where they come from, their job, why they have come on the course and something about themselves (family, hobbies/sports). Emphasize that at this point they should not talk about jobs in detail. Set a time limit of 10 minutes total, and check after 5 minutes that students have swapped asking and answering. Circulate, encourage the students and help with vocabulary.

2 (Option continued) Ask every student to briefly introduce their partner to the group. Write new vocabulary on the board as it is used or needed (countries, job titles etc.), and make a note of good/bad language use. After each introduction invite the group to ask the introduced student a few questions directly. Break the ice by asking friendly questions yourself or by responding naturally to things that are said.

3 (Option continued) Hold a short feedback slot. It is important to establish right at the start of the course how you will do grammar, vocabulary and pronunciation diagnostically.

4 (Option continued) Do any housekeeping you need to: course information etc.

5 Give out a copy of the worksheet to every student and ask them to look at **section A**. Refer to the instructions. Divide the class into pairs, start the activity and circulate.

ANSWERS

1 leaders **2** main **3** involved **4** per
5 customers/clients ('customer' is also used in shops and restaurants) **6** in charge **7** responsible **8** deal
9 freelancer **10** unemployed/graduated **11** in
12 on

6 Refer to the instructions for **section B**. Allow a few minutes for the students to make notes individually, and emphasize that they should write a few words only. When the students are ready, ask each in turn to briefly present their own company and job. Invite other students to ask questions, and ask some yourself. Write new vocabulary on the board as it is used or needed, and make a note of good/bad language use.

7 Hold a short feedback slot.

8 (Option) Give out the **Needs Analysis** from the front of this Resource Pack and ask students to fill in the 'Communication Skills' and 'Business Topics' sections individually. While students are doing this write up on the board the list of skills and topics. Take whole-class feedback by asking each student in turn to give their scores for the skills and say which topics they are interested in. Write the scores on the board and tick the topics. At the end use the board results to discuss and negotiate the course programme with the students. Finish the discussion by using the Needs Analysis to talk about their expectations for grammar input (by now they will have seen examples of diagnostic language input at stages 3 and 7) and any other objectives they have.

8.1
Your company and job

Worksheet

A Fill in the gaps using words from the box.

> clients   graduated   main   in charge   freelancer   responsible
> customers   involved   leaders   deal   unemployed   per

My company

1 We are a very large company. In fact, we are the _____ in the market.

2 Our _____ competitors are ...

3 We make ... / offer ... / are _____ in various business activities.

4 We produce 4000 tons a / _____ day.

5 Our main _____ (products) / _____ (services) are ...

6 We have a separate department _____ of after-sales service.

My job

7 I'm _____ for ... (main areas of work, people you supervise)

8 I _____ with ... (areas of work, people outside the company)

9 I'm a _____ , I work on short-term projects for a number of clients.

10 I'm _____ at the moment. I _____ in July.

Choose the correct preposition.

11 A company is *in / on* the market.

12 A product is *in / on* the market.

B Talk about your company and job. First make some notes.

- What is the name of your company? Where is your Head Office?

- What is the size of your company? In which countries do you operate?

- What are your main products/services?

- What are your most important markets?

- Who are your main competitors?

- What is your position in the company?

- What are your main responsibilities?

- Are you currently working on any special projects?

► **PHOTOCOPIABLE**

8.2

Selling your products

AIM

To practise discussing the features, price, availability, after-sales service and terms of payment of the students' own products.

TIME

50–60 minutes

PREPARATION

Make one copy of the worksheet for each student in the class.

PROCEDURE

1 Write up on the board the heading *Selling your products* and underneath, scattered randomly, the ten bulleted items in section C of the worksheet (exclude 'any other relevant information'). Check the meaning of every item ('feature' = an interesting and important part of a product; 'terms of payment' = conditions of payment, i.e. the clause in the contract that says exactly when and how the money will be paid). Then write the numbers 1 to 10 on the board. Divide the class into pairs and ask them to think of a likely order for the ten items in a typical sales conversation. Explain that there is no one correct answer. Start the activity and circulate.

2 Have a brief whole-class discussion to review ideas. Fill in the numbers 1–10 with an order that the majority of the group are happy with, but say again that it is only one possible order and there is no right answer. (One possible order is shown in section C of the worksheet, working down the columns).

3 Give out a copy of the worksheet to every student and ask them to look at **section A**. Refer to the instructions. Divide the class into pairs, start the activity and circulate.

ANSWERS

1 feature – b) requirement – d) specifications – a)
   characteristic – e) USP – c)
2 an estimate – c) a quotation – a) a budget – b)
3 value for money
4 warranty/inventory
5 credit period
6 a) terms b) on c) balance d) additional
   e) settle (= to pay in full what is owed)
   f) invoice (= a bill for goods sent or work done)

4 Ask students to write a version of the statement in question 6 that is true for first-time customers buying their own products. Take class feedback and discuss differences and what it depends on etc.

5 Refer to the instructions and questions for **section B** Develop a class discussion. (The third bullet point means that sales people should listen closely to what their customers need and ask them questions, rather than starting immediately with sales talk.)

6 Refer to the instructions and role notes for **section C**. Emphasize that Student A will only talk about one specific product/service, and that it is not a full negotiation. Ask all the students to work individually to prepare their turn as Student A, choosing a product and making notes under the various bullet points. Allow 5 minutes for this. Circulate and help with vocabulary.

7 Divide the class into pairs and appoint As and Bs in each pair. Ask Student A to tell Student B what the product is. Remind the students to change roles when they finish and set a time limit of 10 minutes each. Start the activity, circulate and make a note of good/bad language use.

8 Hold a short feedback slot.

CULTURAL HINTS

▼ In America business relationships are friendly and informal, but a continuing personal relationship with individuals is not important. Much business is done over the phone. The selling style is more of a 'hard sell': strong, persuading with facts and figures, using slogans and talking tough.

▼ In Latin America and southern Europe personal relationships are very important. There is a preference for doing business face-to-face. The selling style is more of a 'soft sell': less aggressive, persuading with reasoned argument, talking diplomatically.

▼ In Japan and south-east Asia business is done on a group basis, although relationships with individuals are important. Often there is an older authority figure who seldom appears. In Japan socializing after work is seen as being important to the business relationship. The selling style is more reserved. There is lots of opportunity to ask questions and decisions take longer.

A Answer the questions and fill in the missing letters.

1 Match the words on the left with the definitions on the right. Be careful – some are very similar.

feature	a) the technical details of a product
requirement	b) an interesting and important part of a product
specifications	c) something that makes your product different to others on
characteristic	the market
unique selling point (USP)	d) something a customer asks for, or needs
	e) a typical quality that makes a product recognizable

2 Match the words on the left with the definitions on the right.

an estimate	a) a fixed price given by a supplier for a certain number of items
a quotation	b) 1 a plan of future spending
a budget	2 an amount of money given for a project
	c) an approximate price (used for home repairs, servicing a car etc.)

3 The relationship between quality and price is called v _ _ _ e f _ _ m _ _ _ y.

4 In American English, 'guarantee' = w _ _ _ _ _ _ y and 'stock' = inv _ _ _ _ _ y.

5 In the phrase 'payment within 60 days', 60 days is the cr _ _ _ _ p _ _ _ _ d.

6 Fill in the missing vowels in the words below.
Our normal (a) t _ rms for first-time customers are 50% (b) _ n order with the (c) b _ l _ n c _
payable within 60 days of delivery. We could offer an (d) _ d d _ t _ _ n _ l 3% discount if you
(e) s _ t t l _ in full on (f) _ n v _ _ c _ _

 B Discuss these points.

- In your business, do you give more emphasis to price or quality? Is it realistic to try to do both?
- In your business, which is more important for a good sales consultant: personality, sales technique or product knowledge? What else is important?
- It is said that when you talk to customers you should have 'big ears and a small mouth'. Do you agree? What does it depend on?
- What have you learnt in your career about how to sell effectively? What advice can you give?

C Work with a partner. Change roles when you finish.

Student A. Choose one product that you sell or one service that you offer. Student B is interested, but will not start a detailed negotiation. Talk about:

- your company and its experience in the market
- the features of the product
- the price
- the quality of the product
- guarantees

- the minimum order
- the availability and delivery times
- the after-sales service
- the packaging and transport
- the terms of payment
- any other relevant information

Student B. In the future you might buy some of Student A's products or use one of his/her services. Ask lots of questions, but don't start a detailed negotiation.

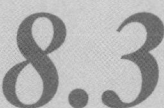

8.3
Trade Fair

Teacher's Notes

AIM

To practise a sales conversation on the stand at a trade fair.

TIME

50–60 minutes

PREPARATION

Make one copy of the worksheet for each student in the class.

In a previous lesson ask the students to bring any realia that they have, i.e. brochures, product samples, etc. Students studying outside their own countries can contact their office and ask for a few key brochure/catalogue pages to be faxed to them.

Be prepared to arrange the desks ('stands') near the edge of the room for the role-play in section C. The company reps. will be behind the desks facing the middle. The visitors will all be in the middle, on chairs facing each stand. Leave as much space as possible between the desks.

PROCEDURE

1 Write up on the board *Trade Fair* and ask students if they attend Trade Fairs, how often, where, how useful they are etc. Students may either attend as visitors or be able to talk about how their own company presents itself on the stand.

2 Give out a copy of the worksheet to every student and ask them to look at **section A**. Refer to the instructions. Divide the class into pairs, start the activity and circulate.

ANSWERS

    a latest/available/range **b** balance **c** imports
    d in full/delivery **e** card **f** in **g** value for money
    h directly **i** helpline **j** look

3 (Option) Practise the target vocabulary by 'pause reading'. Ask students to turn over their sheets. Read each phrase containing a gap saying 'mmm' for the gap. Give enough context, including a few words after each gap if necessary, e.g. for (a) say 'Here's our mmm model'. The students supply the missing word/s chorally.

4 Refer to the instructions for **section B**. Divide the class into pairs, start the activity and circulate.

ANSWERS

    1 c **2** e **3** f **4** a **5** g **6** j **7** b **8** d **9** h **10** i

5 Refer to the instructions and role notes for **section C**. First make sure that everyone knows what they are going to sell on their stand. If someone is a student in real life they could sell something in the room or be the Marketing Officer for their course. If someone is unemployed in real life they could sell something in the room, or think of their last job, or sell their skills on a freelance basis. Then check the instructions: the company reps. stay where they are and receive several visitors one after the other. The visitors keep circulating. Tell the students that they will all have a chance to be company reps.

6 Ask the students to help you arrange the room as in 'Preparation' above. Divide the students into equal numbers of company representatives and visitors. If you have an odd number of people, two visitors can go round together. Ask the company reps. to sit behind a stand waiting for their visitors, who all start together in the middle. Start the activity, circulate and make a note of good/bad language use. You may have to prompt visitors to finish and move on if the circulation doesn't happen naturally.

7 Use your judgment to decide whether to stop the activity after some time and change roles or leave the change of roles until the next lesson. Remember also that it is not necessary for every visitor to visit every stand, although this often works well and gives the students lots of very valuable practice.

8 Hold a short feedback slot.

8.3
Trade Fair

A You might hear the phrases below at a Trade Fair. Try to guess the missing words.

a Yes, here's our la _ _ _ t model. You can see the quality. They're av _ _ _ _ _ _ e in a r _ _ _ e of colours.

b Our normal terms for first-time customers are 50% on order, with the ba _ _ _ _ e payable within 60 days.

c Yes, I'm interested in your food processors. I work for a company that im _ _ _ _ s catering equipment.

d Of course. We can give you 3% if you pay i _ f _ _ l on del _ _ _ _ y .

e Thank you very much, white, no sugar. Here's my c _ _ d.

f Of course, here you are. As you can see, our customers are some of the biggest _ _ the market.

g Well, this one here is excellent va _ _ _ f _ _ m _ _ _ y.

h We can supply di _ _ _ _ ly from stock. Our normal delivery time is 2 weeks.

i We have a customer he _ _ l i _ e, and if we can't deal with the problem over the phone our local agents can respond within 24 hours.

j Let me see, I'll just l _ _ _ it up. Right, that gives a price of 56 dollars a piece.

B Match the questions below with the responses in section A.

1 Can I help you? ___c___

2 Please sit down. Would you like a cup of coffee? I'm sorry, I didn't catch your name. _____

3 Can you give me a list of your main customers? _____

4 Do you have any samples? _____

5 Do you have any cheaper items? _____

6 Could you give me a quotation for 500 pieces? _____

7 What are your terms of payment? _____

8 Do you offer a prompt payment discount? _____

9 What is your usual delivery time? _____

10 What kind of after-sales service do you have? _____

C You are all at a Trade Fair.

Company representatives. You have your own stand. Welcome your visitors and talk about your company and products. If possible, represent your real company and sell your real products. If not, sell something in the room or an object that you have with you.

Visitors to the Fair. Circulate around the stands, asking for information and finding out more about the activities of each company. If another visitor wants to come to the stand where you are talking, finish the conversation quickly but naturally and go to another stand.

▶ **PHOTOCOPIABLE**

8.4a
Dealing with complaints

AIM

To practise dealing with complaints: asking questions, apologizing and giving reasons, offering solutions.

TIME

50–60 minutes

PREPARATION

Make one copy of the worksheet (two pages) for each student in the class.

If possible, set up a telephone and a recording device for sections E and F.

PROCEDURE

1 Write up on the board *Dealing with complaints*. Ask students if their company has a standard policy for dealing with complaints, if the staff who handle complaints are given training, if they themselves ever handle complaints etc.

2 Give out a copy of the worksheet to every student and ask them to look at **section A**. Refer to the instructions. Divide the class into pairs, start the activity and circulate.

ANSWERS

1 handling   2 sample   3 batch
4 mistake /processed   5 credit   6 matter
7 properly   8 inconvenience
9 fault/repair   10 isolated/record
Customer phrases are 3, 7, 9.
Supplier phrases are 1, 2, 4, 5, 6, 8, 10.

3 (Option) Practise the target vocabulary by 'pause reading'. Ask students to turn over their sheets. Read each phrase containing a gap saying 'mmm' for the gap. Give enough context, including a few words after each gap if necessary, e.g. for (2) say 'Could you give me a mmm of the faulty product?'. The students supply the missing word/s chorally.

4 Refer to the instructions for **section B**. Allow 10 minutes for the students to write individually. Circulate, helping with vocabulary.

5 Refer to the instructions for **section C**. Divide the class into pairs. Ask the students in each pair to exchange papers and allow time for them to read their lines and check with their partner anything they don't understand. Remind the students to take turns being customer-complainers (i.e. change roles after every conversation, not at the end of the block of complaints) and to develop the conversation a little each time. The customer-complainers keep and read from their partner's paper, so the supplier-replies are all made without reading. Start the activity, circulate and make a note of good/bad language use.

6 (Option) Ask the best pair/s to re-enact one of the role-plays for the class.

7 Hold a short feedback slot.

8.4a
Dealing with complaints

A Fill in the gaps using words from the box.

> mistake   batch   properly   repair   matter   sample   handling
> isolated   credit   record   processed   inconvenience   fault

1 I'm sorry, it's not our responsibility. The problem must be due to bad _____ .

2 Could you send me a _____ of the faulty product?

3 All these products have the same problem. They all come from the same _____ .

4 I really am very sorry. Our Accounts Department made a small _____ when they _____ your order.

5 If you return it, we'll send a replacement immediately or give you a _____ note.

6 I'm just calling to let you know that our Production Manager is looking into the _____ at the moment, and he'll call you tomorrow.

7 The machine isn't working _____

8 I'm sorry again for any _____ we have caused.

9 This machine has a _____ . How long will it take to _____ it?

10 It must be an _____ case, we have a very good _____ for quality.

Write C next to phrases said by a customer. Write S next to phrases said by a supplier.

B Think of three complaints that a customer might make about your products/services. Write the customer's actual words. Write your replies for each complaint.

1 Complaint: _____

_____

Reply: _____

_____

2 Complaint: _____

_____

Reply: _____

_____

3 Complaint: _____

_____

Reply: _____

_____

C Exchange this paper with a partner who now becomes your customer. Take turns to be customer (who reads the complaints) and supplier (who deals with them). Continue each conversation until the customer is happy.

8 Refer to the instructions for **section D** and to the main headings in the table. Divide the class into pairs, start the activity and circulate. Make sure that students write the sentences in full.

ANSWERS

a) Could you send me a sample of the faulty product?
b) I'm sorry, it's not our responsibility. The problem must be due to bad handling.
c) I really am very sorry. Our Accounts Department made a small mistake when they processed your order.
d) If you return it, we'll send a replacement immediately or give you a credit note.
e) I'm sorry again for any inconvenience we have caused.
f) I'm just calling to let you know that our Production Manager is looking into the matter at the moment, and he'll call you tomorrow.

9 Refer to the two bullet points under the table. Take class feedback.

ANSWERS

First bullet: 3 examples in total (I'll, we'll, he'll)
Second bullet: I'll look into it and get back to you.

10 (Option) Ask the students to turn over their sheets and drill (chorally/individually) some of the fixed expressions. The phrase 'Can you leave ... back to you' is particularly useful and worth memorizing. Drill the phrase by back-chaining:
– *I'll get back to you.*
– *I'll look into it and get back to you.*
– *Can you leave it with me?*
– *Can you leave it with me? I'll look into it and get back to you.*
Tell the students that you want them all to memorize it for homework and then say it fluently at the start of the next lesson.

11 Refer to the instructions and role notes for **section E**. Allow time for students to read and understand the situations. Remind them that they can personalize the calls by deciding together on the product and inventing details. Divide the class into pairs and appoint the customer and supplier for call 1. Ask the students to sit back to back (or use a telephone if you have this facility). If back to back, then ask the students to use the standard 'telephone mime' of a raised hand with thumb up next to the ear and little finger out next to the mouth. Start the activity, circulate and make a note of good/bad language use. Remind students to change roles (each student deals with two complaints).

12 (Option) Ask the best pair/s to re-enact one of the role-plays for the class.

13 Hold a short feedback slot.

14 (Option for next class as recycling) Refer to the instructions for **section F**. Divide the class into new pairs: people who have not worked together recently. Ask the students in each pair to exchange papers like they did before and allow time for them to read their lines and check with their partner about anything they don't understand. Remind the students to take turns initiating calls as customer-complainers. Ask the students to sit back to back (or use a telephone if you have this facility). Start the activity, circulate and make a note of good/bad language use.

15 (Option) Ask the best pair/s to re-enact one of the role-plays for the class.

16 Hold a short feedback slot.

8.4b
Dealing with complaints

Worksheet

D Complete the table by writing supplier phrases 1,2,4,5,6 and 8 from section A in the correct category.

Ask questions	Is it still under guarantee? (a) _____
You are unable to help	We can't really help you, I'm afraid. Have you tried contacting the insurance company? (b) _____ _____
Apologize and explain	Really? Right, I see, I'm very sorry. This has never happened before. It's probably just a computer error. (c) _____ _____
Promise action	Can you leave it with me? I'll look into it and get back to you. (d) _____ _____
End a phone call	If you have any more problems, please let me know. (e) _____
Make a follow-up call	I can assure you we're doing everything we can. (f) _____ _____

• Notice how you use *will*, in its abbreviated form, to promise action. How many examples can you find in the phrases above?

• Find a phrase in the table that means *I'll investigate the problem and I'll call you again.*

E Work with a new partner and make four telephone calls. Take turns to be customer and supplier. Before each call, decide together what the product is. The supplier may have to make a follow-up call if he/she can't deal with the problem immediately

1 **Customer:** You ordered 2000 pieces. This morning 1000 were delivered.
  Supplier: Your factory is very busy at the moment.

2 **Customer:** You received all the goods you ordered, but some are damaged.
  Supplier: The goods were in perfect condition when they left your factory.

3 **Customer:** You received delivery of some machines this morning. You have tested one of the machines and it is not working properly.
  Supplier: Your machines are excellent quality and it is very rare to have problems. You have a technician available but he has a full schedule tomorrow.

4 **Customer:** You recently received delivery of 5000 items. This morning the invoice arrived in the post and there is a mistake.
  Supplier: You recently installed some new accounts software in your computers. Your staff are being trained how to use it at the moment.

F Practise the situations in section B again. Work with a new partner and this time make telephone calls.

▶ **PHOTOCOPIABLE**

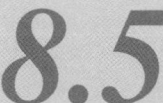

8.5

The business environment

AIM

To practise talking about trends in company structure and culture, and to analyze the sociological, technological, economic and political factors that affect business.

TIME

40–50 minutes

PREPARATION

Make one copy of the worksheet for each student in the class.

PROCEDURE

1 Write up on the board *The business environment* and underneath the seven trends in bold from section A of the worksheet. Have a very brief whole-class discussion to check meanings and establish the general issues.
   - 'Outsourcing'. If a service is provided or a component is made better and more cheaply by an outside company, then it is outsourced to that company.
   - 'Core activities' are the central/main/key activities of a company ('core' = the hard, central part of some fruits e.g. apples).
   - 'An internal market' is where a part of a company provides a competitive service to another part of the same company. For example recruitment or component-making can be done either internally or externally.
   - 'Downsizing' is a reduction in the number of employees in a company and results from competitive pressure in the world market. The remaining full-time employees focus on the company's strengths and most profitable areas (the core activities).
   - 'Delayering' is a reduction in the number of levels in the management structure and produces flexibility and speed of response in a competitive world market, as well as reducing costs.
   - 'Empowerment' = 'giving power'. In this case layers of middle management disappear and lower level staff take on more responsibilities.
   - 'e-commerce' is also called 'e-business' and refers to the whole range of ways that the Internet is used by a company. The 'e' stands for 'electronic'.

The main disadvantages of outsourcing, downsizing and delayering are:
   - They demoralize staff as employees are always worried about job security (although jobs are created in the smaller outsourcing companies).
   - There are fewer opportunities for promotion because of the smaller number of middle managers.
   - It becomes difficult to develop and maintain a company culture as staff turnover is much higher with the more flexible labour market.

2 Give out a copy of the worksheet to every student and ask them to look at **section A**. Refer to the instructions. Explain that you want the students to think about how the changes are affecting their own companies. Allow 10 minutes for the students to read through individually, make a few notes and add an idea of their own. When they are ready, divide the class into small groups and ask them to discuss all the points. Circulate and make a note of good/bad language use. Have a brief whole-class discussion to review ideas at the end.
3 Hold a short feedback slot.
4 (Homework) Refer to the instructions and notes for **section B**. Check all the vocabulary. Explain that you want the students to prepare a mini-presentation on this topic for homework. They will give their presentations in the next lesson. Set a time limit of 10 minutes for the presentations.
5 On the day of the presentations, allocate reasonable time for each presentation as students invariably go over time and there will be questions. At the end of each presentation ask a first question yourself if necessary to get the ball rolling. Consider writing individual feedback sheets during the presentation.

CULTURAL HINTS

▼ In America and northern Europe people live to work. Work provides an opportunity for success through hard work and creativity. Individual achievement is valued.
▼ In Latin America and southern Europe people work to live. Work provides an opportunity for increased status, honour and social recognition. Family security is valued.
▼ In Japan and south-east Asia work provides a sense of identity through membership of a company. Work provides opportunities for success through teamwork. Harmony is valued.

8.5
The business environment

Worksheet

 Is your company changing in response to the changing business environment? Decide which of the following trends are relevant to your business and make a few notes. Add an idea of your own at the end. Then discuss your ideas.

- **Outsourcing.** Has your company outsourced (*subcontracted to an outside company*) any jobs that were previously done internally? What happened?

- **Focusing on core activities.** Is your company diversified into many areas? Or does it focus on a few core (*central*) activities, the things it does best and which are most profitable? Has your company sold off any parts of its business which are not central?

- **The development of an internal market.** Are you in competition with any external companies (outsourcers) to provide a service for your own company? Are you in competition with anyone from your own company?

- **Downsizing.** Has your company gone through a period of downsizing (*reduction in the number of employees*)? What were the benefits and disadvantages? Are only the core staff left? Are other staff employed on a short-term, project-by-project basis? What are the benefits and disadvantages?

- **Delayering.** Has your company gone through a period of delayering (*reduction in the number of levels in the management structure*)? What were the benefits and disadvantages?

- **Employee empowerment.** Do you have 'command and control' type management? Or do you have employee empowerment where responsibility and power are given to lower management levels? What are the benefits and disadvantages?

- **e-commerce.** How is your company taking advantage of the opportunities provided by the Internet? How is your Website integrated into your other business activities? Do you have an e-commerce strategy?

- ?

 Your business is influenced by developments outside business. It is common to analyze these with a STEP analysis. Prepare and present a STEP analysis of how the business environment influences your company.

Sociological factors
Social and cultural attitudes to your type of product; Educational/cultural level of the population; Age of population; Standard of living; Industrial relations

Technological factors
R&D level and 'know-how'; Computerization; Telecommunications; Internet; Other new technologies; Patents; Production methods; Automation; Transport and distribution system

Economic factors
National: Economic growth (GDP); Currency fluctuations; Inflation; Interest rates; Job security and unemployment; Cost of raw materials
World: Patterns of international trade; Moving production sites; Emerging markets

Political factors
Government policy; Government regulations; Privatization; Employment law; Regulatory bodies; Special interest groups (lobbies); International relations; Corruption

▶ **PHOTOCOPIABLE**

8.6

Image, quality, value

AIM

To practise talking about products in terms of brand image, marketing, quality, customer service and customer requirements.

TIME

40–50 minutes

PREPARATION

Make one copy of the worksheet for each student in the class.

PROCEDURE

1 Write up the names of some well-known international companies, e.g. McDonalds, Canon, Gucci, Disney, American Express, BMW, Merrill Lynch, Marks and Spencer, Sony, Arthur Anderson, Benetton, Swatch. Ask what these companies have in common, and why they are successful. Elicit that, amongst other things, the companies all have a strong 'brand image' ('brand' = a product or company name that is well-known).

2 Give out a copy of the worksheet to every student and ask them to look at **section A**. Refer to the instructions. Allow 10 minutes for the students to read through individually and make a few notes. When they are ready, divide the class into small groups and ask them to discuss all the points. Circulate and make a note of good/bad language use. Have a brief whole-class discussion to review ideas at the end.

3 Hold a short feedback slot.

4 (Homework) Refer to the instructions and notes for **section B**. Check the vocabulary ('tailor-made' = customized, personalized). Explain that you want the students to prepare a mini-presentation on this topic for homework. They will give their presentations in the next lesson. Set a time limit of 5 minutes for the presentations.

5 On the day of the presentations, allocate reasonable time for each presentation as students invariably go over time and there will be questions. At the end of each presentation ask a first question yourself if necessary to get the ball rolling. Consider writing individual feedback sheets during the presentation.

8.6
Image, quality, value

Worksheet

A Read the following comments and questions. Decide which are relevant to your company and make a few notes. Then discuss your ideas.

1 A *brand* is a product or company with a well-known name. If a product has a good *brand name* or a company has a strong *brand image* then it has an advantage over its competitors.
- Are your products well-known brands?
- What image does your company have?
- What strategies do you have to develop your brand image?

2 Advertisers try to create an association between buying a product and buying a feeling or lifestyle. For example, when you choose a Land Rover car, you are buying freedom, adventure and independence.
- Do you use advertising that is designed to sell a lifestyle or develop a brand image rather than just give information?
- What feeling or lifestyle do customers 'buy' when they buy your products?

3 Some businesses compete on price, others on quality.
- When your customers say that they are looking for *quality* in the product or service that you offer, what exactly do they mean?
- How do you convince them of the quality of your products?

4 In most areas of modern business there are many similar companies selling similar, high-quality products. To survive you have to compete on customer service and added value. For example, when you go into McDonalds you don't just expect a hamburger. You expect quick service, friendly employees, a clean restaurant, a convenient location and free parking. These are as much a part of the McDonalds product as the hamburger.
- What do your customers expect, *in addition to* your basic product?
- What aspects of your customer service procedures give you an advantage over your competitors?

B Do you think this comment is true? Prepare a mini-presentation, giving examples from your own company.

In modern business it is not enough to sell products, you have to sell solutions. So standardized products are becoming less common. Instead, products are being tailor-made to the customer's exact requirements.

WORKSHEET 8.7

This worksheet is only suitable for middle/senior managers with a good overall knowledge of their company.

AIM

To practise talking about company strengths: procedures, product quality, after sales.

TIME

40–50 minutes

PREPARATION

Make one copy of the worksheet for each student in the class.

Consider which of the two procedures below you will use.

PROCEDURE (CLASSWORK)

1 Write up on the board the phrase *Competitive advantage*. Elicit the meaning (something that helps your company to be more successful than the competitors). Ask students for a few ideas of what gives their own company a competitive advantage.

2 Give out a copy of the worksheet to every student. Refer to the instructions and notes. Check all the vocabulary. Allow 10 minutes for the students to read through individually, make a few notes and add an idea of their own. When they are ready, divide the class into small groups and ask them to discuss all the points. Circulate and make a note of good/bad language use. Have a brief whole-class discussion to review ideas at the end.

3 Hold a short feedback slot.

ALTERNATIVE PROCEDURE (INDIVIDUAL HOMEWORK)

1 As above.

2 Refer to the instructions and notes. Check all the vocabulary. Explain that you want the students to prepare a mini-presentation on this topic for homework. They will give their presentations in the next lesson. Set a time limit of 10 minutes for the presentations.

3 On the day of the presentations, allocate reasonable time for each presentation as students invariably go over time and there will be questions. At the end of each presentation ask a first question yourself if necessary to get the ball rolling. Consider writing individual feedback sheets during the presentation.

8.7
Competitive advantage

Why should customers choose your company rather than your competitors? Decide which of the following areas are relevant to your business and make a few notes. Add an idea of your own at the end. Then discuss your ideas.

- **Physical space.** Front office; Reception area; Sales area

- **Public relations.** Employee attitude and helpfulness; Employee appearance

- **Initial procedures.** Filling in forms; Establishing needs; Advice; Follow-up

- **Ordering.** Acknowledgment of order; Procedure if agreed conditions have to be changed

- **Information.** Detailed product information; Clear instructions for use; Clear invoicing

- **Product quality.** Composition/Ingredients; Active life; Running costs; Environmentally friendly

- **Customization.** Ability to customize your products to the customer's specific requirements

- **Packaging and design.** Styling; Design; Size; Colour; R&D (research and development) input

- **Additional services.** Guarantees; Service contracts; Training in how to use and maintain the product

- **Customer Service.** After-sales access; Telephone help; Maintenance and servicing

- **Financial.** Payment; Flexibility of terms

- ?

8.8

Market profile for consumer products

Teacher's Notes

WORKSHEET 8.8

This worksheet is only suitable for managers with some knowledge of the marketing strategy of their company and whose products sell to the general public, not other businesses.

AIM

To practise talking about the target market and the buying behaviour of consumers.

TIME

40–50 minutes

PREPARATION

Make one copy of the worksheet for each student in the class.
Consider which of the two procedures below you will use.

PROCEDURE (CLASSWORK)

1 Draw on the board a target with concentric circles and in the middle write the words *target market*. Elicit the meaning (the market which you are trying to reach). Ask the students what the target market for their products is.

2 Give out a copy of the worksheet to every student. Refer to the instructions and notes. Check all the vocabulary. Allow 10 minutes for the students to read through individually, make a few notes and add an idea of their own. When they are ready, divide the class into small groups and ask them to discuss all the points. Circulate and make a note of good/bad language use. Have a brief whole-class discussion to review ideas at the end.

3 Hold a short feedback slot.

ALTERNATIVE PROCEDURE (INDIVIDUAL HOMEWORK)

1 As above.

2 Refer to the instructions and notes. Check all the vocabulary. Explain that you want the students to prepare a mini-presentation on this topic for homework. They will give their presentations in the next lesson. Set a time limit of 10 minutes for the presentations.

3 On the day of the presentations, allocate reasonable time for each presentation as students invariably go over time and there will be questions. At the end of each presentation ask a first question yourself if necessary to get the ball rolling. Consider writing individual feedback sheets during the presentation.

8.8
Market profile for consumer products

Worksheet

What is the profile of your target market? What is the buying behaviour of your customers? Decide which of the following categories are relevant for your business and make a few notes. Add an idea of your own at the end. Then discuss your ideas.

- **Gender** Male/Female. Who is the end-user? Who is the decision-maker?

- **Socio-economic group** What social class do your consumers belong to? What is the income of your target customer? Are your products up-market, mid-market or down-market? The following factors may be of interest: rank/position at work, type of work, number of people supervised, size of organization, qualifications.

- **Occupation** This is usually considered as a part of socio-economic group, but sometimes a market can be identified with an occupational sector, e.g. teachers, doctors, engineers etc. Is this true for your market?

- **Life cycle** Can you categorize your consumers according to age/stage in life? How does this influence their buying behavior? One set of categories used in marketing is: *bachelor* (young, single, living away from home); *newly married couple* (young, no children); *full nest I, II and III* (couple with children at different ages); *empty nest I* (older married couples, no children at home); *empty nest II* (older couple, retired); *solitary survivor* (in labour force or retired)

- **Children in household** The presence of children in a household affects disposable income, lifestyle, attitudes, consumption patterns etc. Is this important in your market?

- **Home ownership** Owning a home results in specific needs and responsibilities. Is this important for your customers?

- **Lifestyle** Is the lifestyle of your target consumer important? Consider: activities (hobbies, clubs, entertainment), interests (home, food, fashion), opinions (politics, economics, education).

- **Location** Urban, suburban, rural etc.

- **Personal financial management** The consumer's approach to credit and money generally. Is this important in your business?

- **Culture** National, ethnic and 'peer group' (for example teenagers being influenced by other teenagers). Does culture affect the buying behavior of your customers?

- **Psychological needs of consumers** One way to classify a market is based on the needs and motivations of different consumers. There are four consumer types: 1. *Mainstreamers* (who are conventional people with a need for security); 2. *Aspirers* (the typical 'yuppie' – they are trying to achieve something in life and need status symbols and the respect of others); 3. *Succeeders* (who have already achieved success and need to be in control of everything); 4. *Reformers* (who want to influence society and need to feel they are doing good – they also need intellectual satisfaction). Is this classification useful in identifying your target market?

- ?

► **PHOTOCOPIABLE**

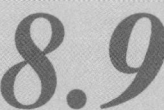
8.9

Selling mobile phones

WORKSHEETS 8.9, 8.10 AND 8.11
These worksheets contain role-plays that could be used in the Telephoning part of a course.

AIM
To practise a sales conversation on the telephone between customer and supplier: features, price, delivery time, terms of payment.

TIME
40–50 minutes

PREPARATION
Make one copy of the worksheet for each student in the class, and fold them across the middle.
If possible, set up a telephone and a recording device.

PROCEDURE
1 Write up on the board *Selling mobile phones*. Ask the group about their own mobile phones: what features do they have? Then explain that the students will work in pairs to have a telephone conversation between a supplier of mobile phones and a customer. Elicit/revise some phrases for a telephone call, such as opening phrases:
   - *Good morning. My name is ... from ... . I'd like some information about ...*
   - *Certainly (name), I'm sure we can help you.*
   And checking and clarifying phrases:
   - *I'm sorry, I don't understand.*
   - *Can you repeat that please?*
   - *So, ... (+ repeat information to confirm)*

2 Set the scene: the supplier represents an international manufacturer of mobile phones. Their latest model 7800 has some very advanced features. The customer represents a company who want to buy a large number of these phones to give to their middle and senior managers for business use. Divide the class into pairs and ask students to choose their role, A (Supplier) or B (Customer).

3 Give out the correct half of the worksheet to each student. Ask pairs of As to sit together, and pairs of Bs to sit together. Allow 10 minutes for these students with the same role to read through their worksheets together and prepare sales information (As) or questions (Bs). Circulate and help with vocabulary.

4 Regroup into the A/B pairs who will do the activity. When the students are ready, ask the pairs to sit back to back (or use a telephone if you have this facility). If back to back, then ask the students to use the standard 'telephone mime' of a raised hand with thumb up next to the ear and little finger out next to the mouth. Start the activity, circulate and make a note of good/bad language use.

5 (Option) Ask the best pair/s to re-enact the role-play for the class.

6 Hold a short feedback slot.

8.9
Selling mobile phones

Worksheet

Student A: Supplier

> You are the Area Sales Manager of Konnekt, an international mobile phone manufacturer. Your best selling phone for business clients is model 7800. It can access the Internet. You will receive a call from a customer who wants to buy a large number of these phones. Before you start, decide on the information below.

- Your company (history? size? experience in the market?)

- Main features of model 7800

- Guarantee

- Price per unit

- Minimum order

- Delivery time

- Terms of payment

--- ✂ ---

Student B: Customer

> Your company wants to give a good quality mobile phone with Internet access to all its middle and senior managers. They need to contact each other and head office easily at all times. You are responsible for seeing what is available. Your first call will be to the Area Sales Manager of Konnekt, an international manufacturer of mobile phones. Call to find out more information about their company, products, prices and terms. Ask lots of questions, but don't enter a detailed negotiation or make any decisions.

Notes

8.10

Selling your products on the telephone

AIM

To practise a sales conversation on the telephone between customer and supplier, based on the supplier's real-life products/services.

TIME

50–60 minutes

PREPARATION

Make one copy of the worksheet for each student in the class, and fold them across the middle.
If possible, set up a telephone and a recording device.

PROCEDURE

1 Explain to the group that they will practise a series of telephone calls between supplier and customer where each student will sell their real-life products/services. Elicit/revise some phrases for a telephone call, such as those given at stage 1 of worksheet 8.9.

2 Set the scene: ask students to think of a real-life product/service to talk about. Remind them that their partner will be from a different business area, and so they should choose something that does not require too much specialist knowledge. Divide the class into pairs, as far as possible putting together students with a similar background, and ask students to choose their role, Supplier or Customer. Tell them that they can change roles later (you could do this in the next lesson).

3 Give out the correct half of the worksheet to each student. Refer to the information in the boxes. Then ask the suppliers to tell the customers which product they are going to talk about, and to give two or three typical questions that their customers often ask. Tell the customers to write this information on their worksheet, and to write the questions as short, simple direct questions that can be used easily during the call. Circulate and help with vocabulary.

4 When the students are ready, ask the pairs to sit back to back (or use a telephone if you have this facility). If back to back, then ask the students to use the standard 'telephone mime'. Refer to the instructions for **Call 1** and remind the customers to ask a lot of questions, not just the ones they have written down. Start the activity, circulate and make a note of good/bad language use.

5 Hold a short feedback slot.

6 Before asking the students to look at Call 2, tell them that there is going to be a problem. Elicit what this is (the customer is going to say no). Discuss with the group how the customer will give this information and how the supplier should respond. Write on the board a few possible phrases such as:

– *I've got some bad news, I'm afraid. My boss has decided not to buy your product/use your service this time. I really am very sorry about this.*

– *I understand. There's no problem. Please feel free to contact me at any time if you change your mind. I hope we can do business in the future.*

7 Ask the students to look at **Call 2**. Give the students time to read their instructions. When they are ready, ask the pairs to sit back to back again (or use the telephone). Start the activity, circulate and make a note of good/bad language use.

8 Hold a short feedback slot.

9 (Now, or in the next-class as recycling) Students change roles and repeat the whole activity. Hold another short feedback slot.

Student A: Supplier

> You will describe your real-life products to a potential customer on the telephone. First tell your partner what type of product/service you are going to talk about, and give him/her some typical questions to ask you. Then receive Call 1.

Call 1 Receive a call from a potential customer who is interested in your products. Try to persuade the customer to buy your product/use your service.

A few days later ...

Call 2 Receive a call from the same customer.

✂ -

Student B: Customer

> You are interested in your partner's real-life products/services and will call him/her on the telephone to find out more information. First prepare the call by talking to your partner and filling in the information below. Then make Call 1.

Type of product/service you will ask about: _____

Question 1 _____

Question 2 _____

Question 3 _____

Call 1 Make a call to your partner. Find out about his/her company, products, prices and terms. Do <u>not</u> make any decision yet – other suppliers have similar products and your boss will make the final decision.

A few days later ...

Call 2 Make a call to the supplier. Your boss has decided not to buy this product/use this service at the moment. Apologize. You will contact them again in the future if the situation changes.

8.11

Apologize, explain and offer

AIM

To practise making and dealing with complaints.

TIME

50–60 minutes

PREPARATION

Make one copy of the worksheet for each student in the class.

If possible, set up a telephone and a recording device.

Consider doing Situations 1–3 in one lesson, and Situations 4–5 in another.

PROCEDURE

1 Write up on the board the heading *Customer complaints*. Tell the students that they will practise some telephone calls between a customer and supplier discussing typical problems with the supply of products. Elicit and write up a short list of possible problems:
   - *goods damaged in transit*
   - *faulty goods*
   - *late arrival of goods*
   - *delivery of the wrong number of goods*
   - *mistakes with the paperwork* etc.

   Then write up the heading *Supplier: dealing with complaints* and underneath the four sub-headings from the worksheet:
   – *Ask questions*
   – *Apologize and explain*
   – *Offer a solution*
   – *End the call*

   Elicit and write up a few phrases for each (see top of worksheet for examples). Depending on how much telephoning practice the students have done, you may have to quickly elicit/revise some phrases for a telephone call, such as those given at stage 1 of worksheet 8.9.

2 Give out a copy of the worksheet to every student. Refer to the instructions and table of useful phrases. Explain that they can use these phrases and the ones on the board if they want to, but it is not necessary. Divide the class into pairs and ask students to look at **Situation 1** and decide who is the customer and who is the supplier.

3 When the students are ready, ask the pairs to sit back to back (or use a telephone if you have this facility). If back to back, then ask the students to use the standard 'telephone mime'. Start the activity, circulate and make a note of good/bad language use.

4 (Option) Ask the best pair/s to re-enact the role-play for the class.

5 Hold a short feedback slot.

6 Refer to the instructions for **Situation 2**. Confirm that there is no connection with the previous role-play and ask the students to change roles and sit back to back again. Start the activity, circulate and make a note of good/bad language use.

7 (Option) Ask the best pair/s to re-enact the role-play for the class.

8 Hold a short feedback slot.

9 Refer to the instructions for **Situation 3**. Discuss with the students what the customer would say in this situation (probably they will have to apologize and offer a solution rather than the supplier). Ask the students to change back to their situation 1 roles and decide what product they are going to talk about. When they are ready they sit back to back again. Start the activity, circulate and make a note of good/bad language use.

10 (Option) Ask the best pair/s to re-enact the role-play for the class.

11 Hold a short feedback slot.

12 (Now, or in the next class as recycling) Ask the students to work with a new partner and then continue with **Situations 4 and 5**. Hold further short feedback slots.

8.11

Apologize, explain and offer

Work with a partner. Take turns to be customer and supplier in the phone calls below. The supplier may decide to make a follow-up call.

Ask questions	Have you tried ... (+ *ing* form of verb)? When did you ...?
Apologize and explain	Really? I'm very sorry, this has never happened before. It's probably just ... We're having a small problem with ... . We're doing everything we can. Our Accounts Department made a small mistake when they processed your order. I really am very sorry.
Offer a solution	No problem. I'll send you a replacement immediately. Can you leave it with me? I'll look into it and get back to you tomorrow.
End the call	I'm sorry again for any inconvenience we have caused. If you have any more problems, please let me know.

Situation 1

Customer: You ordered some expensive items (you decide what). When you opened the package this morning one of them had a fault.

Supplier: You can send a replacement.

Situation 2

Customer: You ordered some software last month. It still hasn't arrived.

Supplier: This new software package has been very popular. You are temporarily out of stock and are waiting for more deliveries.

Situation 3

Customer: You ordered some products (you decide what – it could be the same as Situation 1). They still haven't arrived.

Supplier: This customer has reached his/her credit limit. Your Accounts Department has told you not to send any more products until the customer's last invoice is paid.

Situation 4

Customer: You recently ordered 10,000 T-shirts from a foreign supplier. 5,000 arrived yesterday and the quality is not as good as the original sample.

Supplier: You manufacture cheap T-shirts in a country with low labor costs. Your success is based on price, not quality. You sent the first half of the order last week. The rest will follow soon, but you can't say exactly when. Your factory is very busy at the moment.

Situation 5

Customer: You recently ordered 15,000 T-shirts from a foreign supplier. They all arrived yesterday but the design on the pocket looks too much like a well-known trademark (you wanted one similar, not the same). Also, there is a small mistake on the invoice.

Supplier: You manufacture cheap T-shirts in a country with low labour costs. As the customer knows, one of the reasons for your success is that your designs are similar to those of well-known brands.

8.12

Dialogue building: selling your products

AIM

To provide a framework for practising a sales conversation of the students' own choice.

TIME

variable

PREPARATION

Make one copy of the worksheet for each student in the class.
Consider which of the two procedures below you will use.

PROCEDURE (INDIVIDUAL HOMEWORK)

1 Tell students that they are going to write a short dialogue based on a typical real-life sales conversation that they have in their job.

2 Give out a copy of the worksheet to every student. Remind them that they should personalize the dialogue as much as possible. Ask them to write the dialogue for homework and bring it to the next lesson.

3 In the next lesson collect in the dialogues and correct them.

4 (Option) Leave one of the dialogues uncorrected, and photocopy one copy of this for each student. In the next lesson ask students to try to correct/improve this dialogue in pairs. In feedback listen to all the suggestions for reformulations and discuss with the class which is the best. Build up the reformulated dialogue on the board line by line. As a round up, practise reading the new dialogue aloud in open/closed pairs, focusing on pronunciation.

ALTERNATIVE PROCEDURE (CLASSWORK)

1 Tell students that they are going to write a short sales dialogue together in pairs. Use any sales dialogue where both students can predict the content. For example:
   - one of the role-plays from this/another book, before doing it as a fluency exercise
   - one of the role-plays from this/another book, after doing it as a fluency exercise
   Note that it is not necessary to write the dialogue with the same partner who was/will be involved in the role-play.

2 Give out a copy of the worksheet to every student. Divide the class into pairs. Explain that the pair will think of and write the dialogue together, and that both students should keep a record of the whole dialogue. Set a time limit for the task (e.g. 30 minutes). Start the activity and circulate.

3 Ask the pairs to practise reading their dialogues together quietly. Then ask the best pair/s to read out their dialogues for the class.

4 (Option) Take the written dialogues from each pair and redistribute them (so the pairs remain the same but they have another pair's dialogue). First ask the students to study their new dialogues together quietly and make sure they can read them. Then ask them to practise reading the dialogues aloud.

Write a short dialogue using the model below.

Customer		**Supplier**
Make inquiries about the company.	◄ ►	Talk about your company.
Explain your needs. / Ask questions.	◄ ►	Ask and answer questions.
Ask about the price and any discounts.	◄ ►	Give information.
Ask about terms of payment.	◄ ►	Give information.
Ask about the after-sales service.	◄ ►	Give information.
Ask about the availability and delivery time.	◄ ►	Give information.
Make an order.	◄ ►	Be helpful.

8.13

Dialogue building: complaining and apologizing

AIM

To provide a framework for practising a complaining and apologizing conversation of the students' own choice.

TIME

variable

PREPARATION

Make one copy of the worksheet for each student in the class.

Consider which of the two procedures below you will use.

PROCEDURE (INDIVIDUAL HOMEWORK)

1 Tell students that they are going to write a short dialogue based on a typical real-life complaint that they have in their job.

2 Give out a copy of the worksheet to every student. Remind them that they should personalize the dialogue as much as possible. Ask them to write the dialogue for homework and bring it to the next lesson.

3 In the next lesson collect in the dialogues and correct them.

4 (Option) Leave one of the dialogues uncorrected, and photocopy one copy of this for each student. In the next lesson ask students to try to correct/improve this dialogue in pairs. In feedback listen to all the suggestions for reformulations and discuss with the class which is the best. Build up the reformulated dialogue on the board line by line. As a round up, practise reading the new dialogue aloud in open/closed pairs, focusing on pronunciation.

ALTERNATIVE PROCEDURE (CLASSWORK)

1 Tell students that they are going to write a short complaining and apologizing dialogue together in pairs. Use any dialogue where both students can predict the content. For example:
   – one of the role-plays from this/another book, before doing it as a fluency exercise
   – one of the role-plays from this/another book, after doing it as a fluency exercise

Note that it is not necessary to write the dialogue with the same partner who was/will be involved in the role-play.

2 Give out a copy of the worksheet to every student. Divide the class into pairs. Explain that the pair will think of and write the dialogue together, and that both students should keep a record of the whole dialogue. Set a time limit for the task (e.g. 30 minutes). Start the activity and circulate.

3 Ask the pairs to practise reading their dialogues together quietly. Then ask the best pair/s to read out their dialogues for the class.

4 (Option) Take the written dialogues from each pair and redistribute them (so the pairs remain the same but they have another pair's dialogue). First ask the students to study their new dialogues together quietly and make sure they can read them. Then ask them to practise reading the dialogues aloud.

8.13
Dialogue building: complaining and apologizing

Write a short dialogue using the model below.

Customer		**Supplier**
Describe a problem with some goods/a service.	◄ ►	Ask questions. Acknowledge the problem and apologize. Explain.
Ask for action.	◄ ►	Agree next steps / Give options / Promise action.

_____

_____

_____

_____

_____

_____

_____

_____

_____

_____

_____

_____

_____

_____

_____

_____

_____

_____

_____

_____

_____

_____

9.1

An introduction to negotiating

Teacher's Notes

AIM

To review negotiating vocabulary and discuss the students' own negotiations.

TIME

30–40 minutes

PREPARATION

Make one copy of the worksheet for each student in the class.

PROCEDURE

1 Write up on the board the phrase *to negotiate a deal* and elicit the meaning of 'deal' (the final agreement). Elicit and write up the phrase used to signal an agreement at the end of a negotiation (*It's a deal*). Say *It's a deal* to the student nearest to you and shake their hand, eliciting *It's a deal* and a handshake back from them. Then ask students to chain the phrase and action round the group.

2 Write up on the board the words *a concession* and *a compromise*. Write up a vertical scale from £90 at the bottom to £100 at the top with gradations every pound. Write *supplier wants* at the top, and *customer wants* at the bottom. Put one finger by the supplier figure and one by the customer figure and move them closer and closer (the supplier says ..., but the customer says ...) until you get to £95. Elicit the meaning of the two words on the board: the concessions (one pound every time) and the compromise (£95).

3 Give out a copy of the worksheet to every student and ask them to look at **section A**. Refer to the instructions. Divide the class into pairs, start the activity and circulate.

ANSWERS

1 d   2 c   3 a   4 b

4 Refer to the instructions for **section B**. Divide the class into pairs, start the activity and circulate.

ANSWERS

1 bargaining   2 high   3 short   4 flexible
5 compromise   6 concessions   7 reduce   8 discount
9 increase   10 outcome   11 terms   12 deal
(Note. 'bargaining' and 'negotiating' are near synonyms, with the former being a little more specific and referring to price and conditions only.)

5 Practise the target vocabulary by 'pause reading'. Ask students to turn over their sheets. Read each phrase containing a gap saying 'mmm' for the gap. Give enough context, including a few words after each gap if necessary, e.g. for (2) say 'A price can be too mmm or too mmm'. The students supply the missing word/s chorally.

6 Refer to the instructions for **section C**. Divide the class into pairs, start the activity and circulate.

ANSWERS

1 b   2 c   3 a   4 e   5 d   6 f   7 i   8 j   9 l   10 g
11 k (premises = workplace)   12 h

7 Refer to the instructions and bullet points for **section D**. Develop a class discussion, writing new vocabulary on the board as it is used or needed.

CULTURAL HINTS

▼ In America and northern Europe less importance is given to social aspects such as protocol, respect for status and connections.

▼ In Latin America and southern Europe more importance is given to these aspects, as well as expressions of hospitality and courtesy of discussion.

▼ In Japan and south-east Asia negotiation is more like a social ceremony. Seating displays a harmonious relationship, for example with people of equal status sitting opposite each other.

9.1
An introduction to negotiating

A Match the words with the definitions:

1	a deal	**a**	something given by one side in order to reach an agreement
2	an outcome	**b**	a mid-position where both sides accept less than they really want
3	a concession	**c**	a result
4	a compromise	**d**	the final agreement at the end of a negotiation

- Notice that we say *to do a deal* (process), *to make a deal* (final result), *to make a concession*, *to reach a compromise* and *to reach an agreement*.

B Fill in the gaps using words from the box.

> discount   outcome   increase   compromise   concessions
> reduce   bargaining   deal   high   short   flexible   terms

The process of making and reacting to offers in a negotiation is often called (1) _____ .
A price can be too (2) _____ or too low. A delivery time can be too long or too (3)
_____ . Terms of payment can be very strict or more (4) _____ . To
reach a (5) _____ , both sides may have to make some (6) _____ .
For example, the supplier might have to (7) _____ the price or increase the (8)
_____ . The customer might have to (9) _____ his order. If the (10)
_____ is successful, both sides will be able to agree (11) _____ and
say *It's a (12)* _____ !

C Commercial negotiations cover a range of areas. Match each area on the left with a definition on the right.

1	prompt payment discount	**a**	a reduction to help launch a new line
2	quantity discount	**b**	a reduction available for pre-payment or payment soon after delivery
3	promotional discount		
4	delivery time	**c**	a reduction available for the purchase of large amounts
5	exclusivity	**d**	sole rights in a geographical area
6	terms of payment	**e**	how long the goods will take to arrive
		f	financial conditions for a sale

7	minimum order	**g**	the cost of delivery
8	guarantee/warranty	**h**	the correct way of doing something
9	length of contract	**i**	the smallest number of items that can be supplied
10	transport costs	**j**	a promise of quality, or that faults will be repaired
11	penalty for late delivery	**k**	an extra discount because the goods arrive at the customer's premises after the agreed time
12	procedure	**l**	how long the business agreement will last

D Talk about the type of negotiations you have in your job.

- What type of negotiations do you have?
- Which negotiating areas in section C are important for you?
- Are there any other areas not included in the list?

 PHOTOCOPIABLE

9.2
Opening the negotiation

AIM

To practise opening strategies in a negotiation, including relationship building and discussing needs and starting positions.

TIME

40–50 minutes

PREPARATION

Make one copy of the worksheet for each student in the class.

PROCEDURE

1 Write up on the board the heading *Opening the negotiation*. Ask the students how they begin a negotiation with someone who they are meeting for the first time. Establish the idea of *relationship building* and write it on the board.

2 Give out a copy of the worksheet to every student and ask them to look at **section A**. Refer to the questions and develop a class discussion. ('Relationship building' typically consists of greeting, offering a drink and small talk about the journey to the meeting etc., followed by a discussion about the history of the two companies, their experience in the market and an exchange of market information.)

3 Refer to the instructions for **section B**. Divide the class into pairs, start the activity and circulate. Check the answers by asking open pairs to read the mini-dialogues.

ANSWERS

1 That seems rather high.   **2** Isn't that a little low?
3 Something nearer 5%.   **4** About six weeks.
5 I didn't expect it to be so long.   **6** Can you tell me about your terms of payment?   **7** What do you mean?
8 We'd prefer, say, 60 days credit.

4 (Option) Elicit/discuss further aspects of the language in the mini-dialogues:

● There is a line-by-line pattern to all four dialogues: after an initial question and factual answer the customer tries to get a concession; the supplier doesn't answer directly but instead asks what the customer wants; finally the supplier says 'no', but clearly leaves open the possibility of further negotiation.

● There is considerable use of tentative, indirect language:
  – second conditional (*If we ordered, ...*)
  – past continuous instead of present continuous (*were you thinking of/looking for*)
  – past simple instead of present simple (*What did you have in mind?*)
  – 'seems' for 'is'
  – 'rather high' and 'a little short'
  – negative questions (*Isn't that a little low? Couldn't you be a little more flexible?*)

5 Refer to the instructions for **section C**. Remind students how the meeting will begin (relationship building) and elicit and write on the board some host phrases:
  – *Come in/Did you have a good flight?/May I take your coat?/Would you like some coffee or mineral water?/What was the weather like in ...?'*
Elicit and write up a phrase for 'getting down to business' such as:
  – *OK. As I said on the phone the other day, ...*
Set up the activity: the meeting takes place in the supplier's country so the supplier is the host. The customer has just arrived from the airport. They have spoken on the phone but have never met. Establish some products that could be used for the negotiation (anything in the room – dictionaries, bottled water, a watch that one of the students is wearing etc.).

6 Divide the class into pairs and let each pair decide who is supplier, who is customer and what product they are going to negotiate about. The customers go outside the classroom and knock on the door in turn. The suppliers stand inside the room by the door, waiting for their visitor. Start the activity, circulate and make a note of good/bad language use.

7 Hold a short feedback slot.

CULTURAL HINTS

▼ In America and northern Europe little time is spent on relationship building.

▼ In Latin America and southern Europe personal relationships are very important. A long time is spent building trust. In South America it is important to show respect for national characteristics.

▼ In Japan and south-east Asia building understanding and group harmony is necessary before any business can be discussed. It is important to show respect for the company.

A The first time you meet someone for a negotiation you spend time 'relationship building'. How important is this in your negotiations? What does it consist of?

B After relationship building the two sides will discuss objectives and starting positions. Below are four separate dialogues about different issues. Fill in the gaps using phrases from the box.

> Something nearer 5%.   Isn't that a little low?   That seems rather high.
> I didn't expect it to be so long.   Can you tell me about your terms of payment?
> What do you mean?   About six weeks.   We'd prefer, say, 60 days credit.

Price

Customer: *What's the cost per item?*
Supplier: *The unit price is 600 dollars.*
Customer: (1) _____
Supplier: *What sort of price were you thinking of?*
Customer: *We were expecting something around 550 dollars.*
Supplier: *I think you'll find our prices are standard for this market.*

Quantity and discounts

Customer: *If we ordered, say, 1000 pieces, what sort of discount would you give?*
Supplier: *Our normal quantity discount is 3%.*
Customer: (2) _____
Supplier: *What kind of discount were you looking for?*
Customer: (3) _____
Supplier: *Well, we don't normally give such large discounts.*

Delivery time

Customer: *What's your usual delivery time?*
Supplier: (4) _____
Customer: (5) _____
Supplier: *What exactly did you have in mind?*
Customer: *We need delivery in 4 weeks. Can you do that?*
Supplier: *That's a little short for us. Our production schedule is very busy at the moment.*

Terms of payment

Customer: (6) _____
Supplier: *30 days after delivery.*
Customer: *Couldn't you be a little more flexible?*
Supplier: (7) _____
Customer: (8) _____
Supplier: *I'm sorry, but we only offer those conditions to regular customers.*

C Work with a partner. Decide who is the supplier and who is the customer. Choose a product (something in the classroom). Start with some relationship building, then move on to negotiate the purchase of a large quantity of this product. Invent all the details you need.

AIM

To practise making and reacting to proposals and closing a negotiation.

TIME

50–60 minutes

PREPARATION

Make one copy of the worksheet for each student in the class.

PROCEDURE

1 Write up on the board the heading *Bargaining* and elicit the meaning (agreeing to do something in return for something else, i.e. the central part of negotiating). Then write up the sub-headings:
 – *Making a proposal*
 – *Reacting: Yes*
 – *Reacting: Maybe*
 – *Reacting: No*
 Elicit some phrases for each heading (e.g. see section B of worksheet) and write them on the board.

2 (Option) Under 'Making a proposal' revise conditionals. Write up on the board:
 – *If we agree to payment of ... , you will have to give us ...*
 – *If we agreed to payment of ... , you would have to give us ...*
 Ask the students to explain the difference. Write up on the board as a summary:
 – *Present tense form (agree/will): real, direct, certain, strong*
 – *Past tense form (agreed/would): imaginary, indirect, uncertain, tentative*

3 Give out a copy of the worksheet to every student and ask them to look at **section A**. Refer to the instructions. Remind the students to summarize frequently during the negotiation and again at the end. Divide the class into pairs and appoint customers and suppliers. Start the activity, circulate and make a note of good/bad language use.

4 Hold a short feedback slot.

5 Refer to the instructions for **section B**. Divide the class into pairs, start the activity and circulate.

ANSWERS

1 to/with 2 what about 3 move on to
4 on condition 5 might 6 must 7 reasons
8 the other points

6 Refer to the instructions for **section C**. Ask pairs of students to read the two mini-dialogues aloud. Point out one or two features (the phrases from the table; the use of tentative language such as might/second conditional/could; the linking of concessions).

7 Refer to the instructions for writing four more mini-dialogues. Remind students that the phrases from the table will help them, and that each dialogue is separate. Divide the class into pairs, start the activity and circulate. When the students finish, ask them to practise speaking their dialogues.

8 (Option) Ask the best pair/s to read their dialogues for the class.

9 Refer to the instructions for **section D**. Divide the students so that they have a new partner and role. Tell the students that they are free to introduce new ideas, and remind them to summarize at frequent intervals and again at the end. Start the activity, circulate and make a note of good/bad language use.

10 Hold a short feedback slot.

CULTURAL HINTS

▼ In America and northern Europe bargaining is an open, direct process with no loss of face if the other person says 'no'. Concessions are freely asked for and given. There is much discussion of facts, figures and money. The individual deal is important – the future is a series of individual deals to be taken one at a time.

▼ In Japan and south-east Asia bargaining in a meeting is often unacceptable as it implies that one side or the other will lose face. It is done in an indirect way, outside the meeting, often by subordinates. Open discussion of short-term profit is seen as vulgar and materialist. The long-term business relationship is important.

9.3

Bargaining and closing

Worksheet

A The table below shows starting positions for two sides in a negotiation about product X. Work with a partner. Negotiate until you reach agreement on all the issues.

	Customer wants	**Supplier wants**
Price	£20 per unit	£22 per unit
Quantity	3000 units a month	4000 units a month minimum
Terms	30 days after delivery	50% with order, 50% after 30 days
Advertising	help with costs of a special promotion	to give no help with the promotion

B Complete the table with words from the box.

on condition   what about   might   must   move on to   to/with   reasons   the other points

Making a proposal		If we ..., you would have to ... If you ..., then we can ...
Reacting	**yes**	OK, we can agree (1) _____ that. Now, (2) _____ the question of ...? Yes, that should be possible. Shall we (3) _____ ...?
	maybe	Yes, we could do that, (4) _____ that you ... Well, that (5) _____ be possible, but we need ...
	no	The problem for us is that ... That would be very difficult for us because ...
	strong no	I'm sorry, that's just not possible. I (6) _____ say 'no', and I'll give you my (7) _____ .
Closing	**If we ...**	If we agree to ... , are you happy with (8) _____ ?
	If you ...	If you can ... , then we can close the deal.
	confirming	OK, it's a deal!

C The mini-dialogues below are based on the negotiation in section A. They use phrases from the table.

Customer: *If you can lower the price a little, then we can look at increasing our order.*
Supplier: *Well, that might be possible, but we need an order of at least 4000 units.*

Supplier: *If we agreed to payment of the full amount after 30 days, you would have to give us a bank guarantee.*
Customer: *OK, we can agree to that. Now, what about the question of some help with our special promotion? Could you help us there?*

Write four similar, separate mini-dialogues based on the negotiation in section A.

1	Customer: make a proposal	Supplier: react (yes)
2	Supplier: make a proposal	Customer: react (no)
3	Customer: make a proposal	Supplier: react (maybe)
4	Supplier: try closing (*If we ...*)	Customer: confirm

D Look at the negotiation in section A again. Work with a new partner and/or change roles. Negotiate until you reach agreement on all the issues.

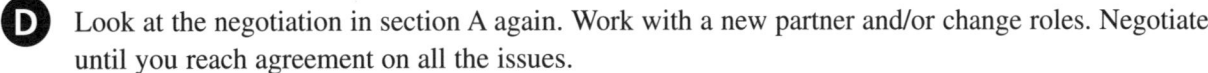

PHOTOCOPIABLE

AIM

To practise a variety of tentative structures including could/would, opening phrases, negative questions and qualifiers in order to speak more carefully in a negotiation.

TIME

40–50 minutes

PREPARATION

Make one copy of the worksheet for each student in the class.

PROCEDURE

1 Write up on the board the heading *Tentative language* and elicit the meaning of 'tentative' (careful, cautious, uncertain). Ask the students what words/techniques they know to make their language more tentative and write up examples (e.g. Maybe, I think etc.).

2 Give out a copy of the worksheet to every student and ask them to look at **section A**. Refer to the instructions. Say the first one or two pairs yourself as a model, then ask individual students to try the other pairs in open class (one student says both sentences in the pair). Refer to the underlining task, divide the class into pairs, start the activity and circulate. When they have finished, the pairs can practise speaking the phrases again, helping each other to sound tentative.

3 Refer to the instructions for **section B**. Check the instructions carefully by referring to the examples that have been done. Divide the class into pairs, start the activity and circulate.

ANSWERS

a 3,4,6　**b** 2,6　**c** 1,4,7　**d** 3,8　**e** 5　**f** 6,8
g 2,5　**h** 1,7

4 Refer to the bullet point question and ask for comments (there is too much tentative language here – it sounds like there is a big problem).

5 Refer to the instructions for **section C**. Divide the class into pairs, start the activity and circulate. When they have finished, ask the students to practise speaking the dialogue together.

POSSIBLE ANSWERS

3 If we bought product X, what terms would you give us?
4 What did you have in mind/What were you thinking of?
5 Could we have a little more credit?
6 That won't be very easy. I'm afraid you're over your limit.
7 To be honest, we have a bit of a problem with our cash-flow at the moment.
8 You can pay some of the money you owe us, can't you?
9 Yes, I think we could probably do that.
10 In that case I think we'd be more flexible.

6 Ask the best pair/s to read their dialogues for the class and write up selected phrases on the board.
7 Refer to the instructions and questions for **section D** and develop a class discussion.

POSSIBLE ANSWERS

First bullet point. Typical situations for tentative language are:
– if the people don't know each other very well (and in general a visitor will use more tentative language than a host)
– if someone is uncertain about a point
– in larger, more formal meetings
– at the beginning of the negotiation
– when it is a national characteristic of the speaker (e.g. the Japanese and the English)

Second bullet point. Students often say at first that tentative language is very 'British English'. However if asked for equivalents of a–h (section B) in their own language they usually find them, with the language used in the same situations.

CULTURAL HINTS

▼ In America language is strong and direct. Confrontation is considered a good thing for progress. The English like a calm, reasonable discussion and use humour freely.

▼ In Latin America and southern Europe expressive and emotive language is common. Grand outlines are talked about at length with the details left to the end.

▼ In Japan, language is indirect and cooperative with many references of appreciation to the other person. Respect for the dignity of others is very important.

9.4
Tentative language

A Practise each pair of sentences. Say the sentences on the left in a strong, clear, direct way. Say the sentences on the right in a tentative, careful, thoughtful way: speak more slowly and use pauses.

1   Our competitors are expensive.   I'm afraid our competitors aren't very cheap.
2   There's a problem with that.   I think there's a bit of a problem with that.
3   It'll be better use Air Express.   Wouldn't it be better to use Air Express?
4   We can't do that.   To be honest, I'm not sure we could do that.
5   There's a misunderstanding.   There seems to be a slight misunderstanding.
6   That's going to be difficult.   I guess that could be a little difficult.
7   That gives us very little time.   Actually, that doesn't give us very much time.
8   The transport costs are expensive.   The transport costs are a bit expensive, aren't they?

Underline all the words in the second column that make the language tentative. The first two have been done for you.

B Complete the table below with the sentence numbers from section A. The first two have been done for you.

a	could/would		**e**	is → seems to be		
b	I think / I guess	2	**f**	a little / a bit (+ adjective)		
c	phrase to introduce bad news	1	**g**	a slight / a bit of a (+ noun)	2
d	negative question		**h**	not (+ opposite)	1

•   What do you think about this example?   *I'm afraid there seems to be a slight problem.*

C Rewrite this dialogue so that it is more tentative. Use techniques from section B and your own ideas.

Customer

1 Product X is very expensive.
3 If we buy product X, what terms will you give us?
5 Can we have more credit?
7 We have a problem with our cash-flow.
9 OK.

Supplier

2 It's more expensive than product Y, but it's much better.
4 What do you mean?
6 That will be difficult. You're over your limit.
8 Pay some of the money you owe us.
10 In that case we'll be more flexible.

Start like this:

1 To be honest, product X seems a bit expensive.
2 It's a little more expensive than product Y, but the quality is better.
3 …

D Discuss:

•   In what situations would you expect to hear tentative language?
•   Do you use tentative structures in your own language?

9.5

Negotiating tactics

AIM

To review a variety of negotiating tactics including choosing to be open or specific during bargaining, linking issues and increasing/decreasing the value of concessions.

TIME

30–40 minutes

PREPARATION

Make one copy of the worksheet for each student in the class.

PROCEDURE

1 Write up on the board the heading *Negotiating tactics* and ask for and write up a few suggestions. You could elicit some of the ideas from the worksheet (see section C a–f and the bullet points in section D).

2 Give out a copy of the worksheet to every student and ask them to look at **section A**. Refer to the instructions then ask one student to read aloud all five examples. Take class feedback on the main difference (they vary in how open or specific the offers and requests are). Then refer to the task underneath the phrases, divide the class into pairs, start the activity and circulate.

ANSWERS

1 b   2 c   3 a   4 e   5 d

3 Refer to the instructions for **section B**. Divide the class into pairs, start the activity and circulate.

ANSWERS

1 a   2 a, b, c ('Supposing', might/could/would, 'perhaps', the second conditional)   3 a, b, c (because early in a negotiation the language is open, flexible and tentative and at the end it is direct and specific)
4 a, b, c, d, e (i.e. all the examples)

4 (Option) Focus on tentative intonation, particularly as revision of worksheet 9.4. In open class ask individual students to say a–c from section A in a careful, thoughtful way (more slowly and with pauses), and d–e in a strong, direct way. Then ask students to practise together in pairs, helping each other with tentative intonation.

5 Refer to the instructions for **section C**. Divide the class into pairs, start the activity and circulate. At the end use the bullet point to develop a class discussion (e.g. about closing tactics such as keeping a final concession 'up your sleeve' in order to close the deal).

ANSWERS

a 2   b 4   c 5   d 1   e 6   f 3
(Note: 'concession' = something given by one side in order to reach an agreement)

6 Refer to the instructions for **section D**. There is no immediate task here, but encourage students to try some of the ideas from the worksheet in future role-plays. At the third bullet point you could ask students what tentative language they remember from worksheet 9.4.

9.5
Negotiating tactics

A The phrases below could all be said by a customer at exactly the same point in a negotiation. What is the main difference between them?

a If we increased our order to 500 units it would mean much more risk for us. We don't know if this product will sell in our market. We would expect a better price.

b Supposing we increased our order? What would be your reaction?

c If you could give us a better price, and perhaps be a little more flexible with your terms, then we might find a way to increase our order.

d If we increase our order to 500 units, will you give us 90 dollars per unit?

e If we increase our order to 500 units, will you give us a better price?

Now put the phrases in sequence, from 1 (the most open and flexible) to 5 (the most direct and specific):

1 _____ **2** _____ **3** _____ **4** _____ **5** _____

B Look back at phrases a–e from Section A. Which phrases:

1 show the customer preparing his/her case with an explanation first?

2 show the use of tentative (uncertain, indirect) language?

3 would you expect to hear nearer to the beginning of the negotiation?

4 show the linking of issues (asking for something in return for giving something)?

C Match examples 1–6 with tactics a–f below.

1 Good, that's a step forward. Shall we move on to talk about the transport arrangements?

2 Well, I could do that, but it would involve some changes to our production schedule.

3 Well, I suppose that helps a little.

4 If we split the shipment in two parts you wouldn't have such high storage costs.

5 Normally we don't do that, but I suppose in this situation it might be possible. I don't know what my boss would say!

6 Let me see. That would save us about 500 dollars a month. At least that's something.

a Emphasizing the 'cost' to you. _____

b Showing how something you want gives them a benefit. _____

c Saying that your concession is not normal. _____

d Moving on quickly after winning a point. _____

e Breaking down large figures to make them seem less. _____

f Devaluing the importance of their concession. _____

• Can you add any other tactics or tricks?

D In your next negotiation remember to:

• Choose carefully whether to be open or specific in your offers and requests

• Link issues

• Use tentative language to show that you are uncertain. (Perhaps you will get an extra concession?)

• Try some of the ideas from section C

▶ **PHOTOCOPIABLE**

9.6
Checking understanding and summarizing

AIM
To practise asking for clarification, paraphrasing and summarizing.

TIME
40–50 minutes

PREPARATION
Make one copy of the worksheet for each student in the class.

PROCEDURE
1 Write up on the board the heading *Checking understanding*. Elicit and write up some phrases (e.g. see worksheet section A). Then write up on the board the heading *Summarizing* and underneath the phrases *Can I just go over/through that again?*. Establish that these both have the same meaning ('go over'/'go through' = look at something carefully, review, recapitulate).

2 Give out a copy of the worksheet to every student and ask them to look at **section A**. Refer to the instructions. Divide the class into pairs, start the activity and circulate.

ANSWERS
1 interrupt   2 detail   3 exactly/by   4 specific
5 saying   6 right   7 correctly

3 Refer to the bullet point. Ask the students if they can see any difference between the two groups (the first four phrases are *asking for more information* and the last three are *using your own words to check understanding*). The students can write these headings on the worksheet.

4 Practise the target phrases by 'pause reading'. Ask students to turn over their sheets. Read each phrase containing a gap saying 'mmm' for the gap. Give enough context, including a few words after each gap if necessary, e.g. for (3) say 'What mmm do you mean?'. The students supply the missing word/s chorally.

5 Refer to the instructions for **section B** and ask the students to do the whole section. Divide the class into pairs, start the activity and circulate.

ANSWERS
1   Summarizing can be used for all the things in the list.
2a   Sorry, can you just go over that again?
2b   Can I just go through those points again?
2c   Can we go over what we've agreed so far?
2d   Let me just check that I understand./Let me just check I understand that.
3   So, ... (followed by a pause)

6 Refer to the instructions and role-notes for **section C**. Check understanding of the activity carefully. (Consider modelling the activity first by asking a good student to be Student A and taking the role of Student B yourself, using language from sections A and B). Typical Student A topics might be: the rules of their national sport; the election system in their country; a complex project they once worked on, etc. Divide the class into pairs and appoint As and Bs. Remind students to change roles when they finish. Start the activity, circulate and make a note of good/bad language use.

7 Refer to the instructions for **section D**. Develop a short class discussion, and refer to any good examples of checking understanding that you heard.

8 Hold a short feedback slot on other language points.

9.6
Checking understanding and summarizing   Worksheet

A These phrases are used for checking understanding. Complete the missing words.

    1 Sorry, can I i _ _ _ _ _ _ _ t? I'm afraid I don't understand.
    2 Sorry, could you explain in a little more d _ _ _ _ l?
    3 I'm sorry, it's still not clear to me. What e _ _ _ _ _ y do you mean _ _ 'a short delay'?
    4 Could you be a little more sp _ _ _ _ c?
    5 Are you s _ _ ing that ... ?
    6 So, in other words, ... Is that r _ _ _ t?
    7 So, if I understand c _ _ _ _ _ _ _ y, we can either ... or ... . Is that right?

• Can you see why the phrases have been put into two groups?

B Summarizing is a useful technique. Answer these questions.

1 Which of the following can 'summarizing' be used for?

    ☐ checking understanding   ☐ keeping a positive atmosphere by reviewing progress

    ☐ giving yourself time to think   ☐ finding a way out of a difficult situation

    ☐ taking the initiative   ☐ preparing to close the negotiation

2 Put these words in the correct order.

    a Sorry, that can just again you over go?

    _____

    b Can go I points through just those again?

    _____

    c Can go far we we've over so what agreed?

    _____

    d Let understand check just I me that

    _____

3 Which two-letter word is often used on its own for summarizing?

C Work with a partner and change roles when you finish.

Student A   Choose a complicated topic that Student B knows nothing about. Talk about it for about five minutes. These phrases will help you:

        Perhaps I didn't make myself clear. What I meant was ...
        I'm sorry, that's not what I meant. If I can put it another way, ...
        I'm afraid there's a slight misunderstanding. What I'm trying to say is ...

Student B   Listen very carefully to Student A. When he/she finishes you have to explain back to him/her what he/she has said. So you should:
       • interrupt regularly to ask questions (see section A)
       • summarize at regular intervals (see section B)

D Discuss how successful you were as Student B in the last activity.

9.7

The negotiating process

WORKSHEET 9.7

This worksheet is only suitable for middle/senior managers involved in negotiating as a regular part of their job.

AIM

To review aspects of the negotiating process by discussing the students' own experience: effectiveness, dealing with people, difficulties, tactics, planning for a forthcoming negotiation.

TIME

40–50 minutes

PREPARATION

Make one copy of the worksheet for each student in the class.

PROCEDURE

1 Give out a copy of the worksheet to every student and ask them to look at **section A**. Refer to the instructions and questions ('outcome' = result). Either develop a class discussion (small groups) or divide the class into twos/threes (larger groups).

2 Refer to the instructions and questions for the whole of **section B**. Either develop a class discussion (small groups) or divide the class into twos/threes (larger groups).

3 (Option) Have an open class round-up of the main points if the students have been working in twos/threes.

4 Refer to the instructions and questions for **section C**. Either develop a class discussion (small groups) or divide the class into twos/threes (larger groups).

5 Refer to the instructions and questions for **section D**. Either develop a class discussion (small groups) or divide the class into twos/threes (larger groups).

6 (Option) Have an open class round-up of the main points if the students have been working in twos/threes.

7 Refer to the instructions and questions for **section E**. Check meaning of a 'win-win' outcome (see Vocabulary Note below). Either develop a class discussion (small groups) or divide the class into twos/threes (larger groups).
Vocabulary Note. The idea of a 'win-win' negotiation is well-known in management. It refers to the fact that negotiations can be a collaborative long-term process where both sides benefit. Techniques to encourage this include showing respect for the other person at all times, being assertive rather than aggressive, not using clever 'tricks' that might backfire or create a bad feeling, giving reasons when you have to say no, etc. This is largely common sense, despite being the subject of numerous books.

8 (Homework) Refer to the instructions and questions for **section F**. Check the meaning of any new words, including the five points in the box ('bottom line' = the least you are willing to accept). Ask the students to make some notes for homework and then give a mini-presentation in the next lesson.

CULTURAL HINTS

▼ In America and northern Europe decisions are made on a short time-scale using facts and numerical information. During bargaining the first offer is within 5–10% of the expected outcome.

▼ In Latin America and southern Europe the decision-making process is longer, and the feelings and intuition of senior managers are also important. During bargaining the first offer is within 20%.

▼ In Japan and south-east Asia there is a long process of collective decision-making based on achieving consensus amongst middle managers. The first offer is very close to the final offer and there is little further bargaining.

9.7
The negotiating process

Worksheet

A Describe a recent negotiation.

- Who was involved?
- What did you negotiate about?
- Was the outcome as you expected? If not, can you explain why?

B Describe a past situation where you feel you were effective as a negotiator. What exactly were you doing that made you effective?

Describe a past situation where you feel you were *not* effective as a negotiator. Can you identify why you were not effective?

C Describe a recent negotiation where you faced a difficult person or situation. How did you deal with things? If you could have the same negotiation again, what would you do differently?

D *'Time and location are crucial factors in a negotiation'.* Do you agree? Can you give an example of where you suffered because you had no control over these factors?

E Some people think of negotiating as a constructive dialogue leading to a 'win-win' outcome. Others think it is basically a battle based on power and tactics.

- What is your approach to negotiating?
- Can you give examples where you have used different approaches?

F Discuss a negotiation that you are going to have in the near future. Make some notes first.

- **Your objectives.** What exactly do you want from the negotiation?
- **Your power.** What power do you have?
- **Their power.** What power does the other side have?

Negotiating theory suggests that there are five basic ways to change the balance of power:
1 the promise of reward
2 the threat of punishment
3 the introduction of new factual evidence
4 the deliberate introduction of distracters such as time deadlines or the intervention of a new person
5 changes in confidence levels

- **Balance of power.** Can you change this?
- **Ideal outcome.** What would be the best possible result? Consider each main issue.
- **Realistic outcome.** Consider this in detail for each issue.
- **Bottom line.** What is the minimum you would accept on each issue?

▶ **PHOTOCOPIABLE**

9.8

Computers

WORKSHEETS 9.8 AND 9.9

Note the following points for supplier/customer negotiating role-plays:

■ Students should have a chance to play both supplier and customer on different occasions.

■ Remember the option of using the same role-play a second time with changed roles and/or partners.

■ Same-role preparation needs to be done out of earshot of the other side. The negotiations themselves also work much better if each pair is in a different room. If this is not possible, create a separate 'space' for each pair by arranging the chairs so that they are facing the corners of the room.

■ Consider a range of feedback methods:
 – closed pairs + teacher (normal: you make language notes for a feedback slot)
 – open pair + class (one pair performs for the class; others watch then comment on language and performance)
 – closed pairs + observers (groups of three: one student sits a little distance away and is an 'invisible observer')

■ If you are working one-to-one, you will have to play one of the roles yourself. Be simple and straightforward, and model lots of target language. Get business ideas from previous students. If you are stuck, ask your student what he/she would do/say in your situation.

AIM

To practise a customer/supplier negotiation based on typical issues such as quantity, price, transport costs, exclusivity and terms of payment.

TIME

50–60 minutes

PREPARATION

Make one copy of the worksheet for each student in the class.

PROCEDURE

1 Write up on the board *New model of computer: the AT–400*. Elicit and write up some of the features of this exciting new model. Tell the students that they are going to practise a negotiation between customer and supplier for the purchase of a large quantity of these computers.

2 Elicit and write up some of the issues that may be discussed during the negotiation (see worksheet main headings). Elicit the different stages of the negotiation, particularly reminding students to begin with relationship building and discussing general objectives before moving on to the detailed bargaining itself.

3 Remind students of any particular language areas from worksheets 9.2 to 9.6 that you want them to focus on.

4 Divide the class into pairs and appoint Customers and Suppliers. Give out the correct half of the worksheet to each student. Group together pairs of students with the same role and ask them to prepare ideas together. Allow at least 15 minutes for this. Circulate, help with vocabulary, and prompt them to discuss:
 – history of their company and experience in the market
 – their ideal outcome, realistic outcome and bottom line for each issue

5 Regroup into the A/B pairs who will do the activity. The supplier is the host and stands by the door, inside the room, waiting for their visitor. The customer has just arrived from the airport and will start the activity outside the classroom. They knock on the door in turn. Start the activity, circulate and make a note of good/bad language use.

6 Hold a short feedback slot.

7 (Now, or in the next-class) The As and Bs change roles and repeat the activity. Hold another short feedback slot.

9.8
Computers

Student A: Customer

> You represent a large chain of computer stores which sells directly to the public. You will meet with a representative of a company that makes computers. You are interested in a new model, the AT-400. Prepare your role carefully before you start.

The following commercial information is confidential.

Quantity	You want to buy 4000 computers as a first order.
Price per unit	You want to pay about £600. You could sell this model to customers for about £1000.
Quantity discount	You expect a discount.
Transport	Are shipping costs included in the price?
Manual	Is it available in your language?
Exclusivity	You want an exclusive agreement in your market. If this is not possible you want to know if other computer stores can sell the AT-400 cheaper than you.
Guarantee	You want a guarantee of 12 months.
Delivery	As soon as possible.
Terms of payment	You are prepared to pay 30% pre-payment, 30% on delivery and 40% 3 months after delivery.

Student B: Supplier

> You represent a company that manufactures and exports computers. Your new model is the AT-400. You will meet with a potential customer who represents a large chain of computer stores. Prepare your role carefully before you start.

The following commercial information is confidential.

Quantity	Your standard minimum order is 5000 computers.
Price per unit	£600 (above £400 is profit for you).
Quantity discount	Negotiable.
Transport	Customer pays. In this case shipping costs will add about 5%.
Manual	Available in translation in all main EU and Asian languages.
Exclusivity	Possible only if customer agrees to order 100,000 units each year for the next three years.
Guarantee	12 months.
Delivery	Goods are shipped about 30 days after a firm order.
Terms of payment	For first-time customers your terms are:

- 50% pre-payment
- 25% on delivery
- 25% 30 days after delivery
- you need a bank guarantee.

For future orders you can be more flexible.

▶ **PHOTOCOPIABLE**

AIM

To practise a customer/supplier negotiation based on typical issues such as choice of product, price, terms of payment and additional services.

TIME

50–60 minutes

PREPARATION

Make one copy of the worksheet for each student in the class.

As an additional help with the lead-in, find a picture of a factory/offices lit at night with stylish modern lighting.

PROCEDURE

1 Write up on the board *Modern lighting design*. Ask students if they know of any buildings, offices or factories with a good lighting design that creates a strong image for the organization or company. Tell the students that they are going to practise a negotiation between customer and supplier for the purchase of a large quantity of lamps for a new factory.

2 Elicit and write up some of the issues that may be discussed during the negotiation (see worksheet). Elicit the different stages of the negotiation, particularly reminding students to begin with relationship building and discussing general objectives before moving on to the detailed bargaining itself.

3 Remind students of any particular language areas from worksheets 9.2 to 9.6 that you want them to focus on.

4 Divide the class into pairs and appoint Customers and Suppliers. Give out the correct half of the worksheet to each student. Group together pairs of students with the same role and ask them to prepare ideas together. Allow at least 15 minutes for this. Circulate, help with vocabulary, and prompt them to think about what they want from the negotiation. In particular, encourage the suppliers to sell their lighting design service.

5 Regroup into the A/B pairs who will do the activity. The supplier is the host and stands by the door, inside the room, waiting for their visitor. The customer has just arrived from the airport and will start the activity outside the classroom. They knock on the door in turn. Start the activity, circulate and make a note of good/bad language use.

6 Hold a short feedback slot.

7 (Now, or in the next-class) The As and Bs change roles and repeat the activity. Hold another short feedback slot.

CULTURAL HINTS

▼ Americans and northern Europeans sit facing each other and maintain eye contact when negotiating. Seating rarely reflects status.

▼ In Latin America and southern Europe eye contact is maintained. Seating usually shows the status of individuals, with the most senior person sitting at the head of the table facing the door.

▼ The Japanese sit side-by-side and stare at a common point, giving sideways glances to their counterparts to check understanding. Seating order round the table may reflect seniority, with counterparts of equal status opposite each other.

9.9
Lamps

Student A: Customer

> Your company is building a big new factory and you need to install a good lighting system. You need 100 lamps to light the area. You will meet a representative of a company that supplies lighting equipment. Prepare your role carefully before you start.

Do some relationship-building, then ask about:

- the supplier's product range
- prices and discounts (another supplier has quoted you £200 per lamp)
- terms of payment
- guarantees and maintenance
- delivery and installation time (the lighting will be needed in about 3 months)
- if they will accept a penalty clause for late installation

Student B: Supplier

> You work for a company that makes high-quality industrial and commercial lamps. You have ISO 9000 (the international guarantee of quality). Your lamps can be found on highways in Finland and in boutiques in Paris and Buenos Aires. You will meet with a potential customer who wants new lamps. Prepare your role carefully before you start.

You have two products to sell:

	Standard model	New model
Special features	——	energy-efficient / longer life
List price (per lamp)	£200	£300
Guarantee	two years	four years

For both models of lamp:

Quantity discount	Negotiable.
Terms of payment	Negotiable, but you expect a good percentage in advance.
Guarantee	See above, and it includes a free inspection every year. Guarantee is renewable for a small cost.
Delivery	3 months (your factory is very busy at the moment).
Installation	This takes another one month after delivery.
Penalty	It is not company policy to have a penalty for late delivery/installation.

Lighting design service. This customer wants a simple internal lighting system. You also offer a lighting design service for the inside and outside of the factory and offices using advanced computer software. Modern lighting design will improve the image of any company. A visit by one of your consultants costs £4,000. The consultant produces a report.

▶ **PHOTOCOPIABLE**

9.10

A salary increase

AIM

To practise an employee/manager negotiation over salary increase and benefits.

TIME

40–50 minutes

PREPARATION

Make one copy of the worksheet for each student in the class.

PROCEDURE

1 Write up on the board the three headings *Salary increase*, *Fringe benefits* and *Training courses*. Elicit the meaning of 'fringe benefit' (an extra benefit given to an employee in addition to salary). Elicit and write up common fringe benefits (these change over time and between countries, but a company car and free health insurance are typical). Ask students what kind of training courses they have been on in the last year or so where their company has paid (e.g. this English course, a computer course etc.). Tell the students that they are going to practise a negotiation between employee and manager for a salary increase and possible fringe benefits and paid training courses.

2 Remind students of any particular language areas from worksheets 9.2 to 9.6 that you want them to focus on.

3 Divide the class into pairs and appoint Employees and Managers. Give out the correct half of the worksheet to each student. Group together pairs of students with the same role and ask them to prepare ideas together. Allow at least 10 minutes for this. Circulate, help with vocabulary, and prompt them to think about what they want from the negotiation. In particular, encourage the employees to think of realistic fringe benefits and training courses.

4 Regroup into the A/B pairs who will do the activity. The manager will stand by the door, inside the room, waiting for their employee. The employee will start the activity outside the classroom. They knock on the manager's 'office door' in turn. Start the activity, circulate and make a note of good/bad language use.

5 Hold a short feedback slot.

6 (Now, or in the next-class) The As and Bs change roles and repeat the activity. Hold another short feedback slot.

Student A: Employee

> Negotiate your salary increase for next year. As always, the economic climate is difficult, but you want a reasonable increase. Prepare your role carefully before you start.
> - You joined the company three years ago.
> - Last year inflation was 5%. Your salary increase was 3%.
> - You have had new responsibilities this year and your department has performed well. Your company believes in motivating good workers – that's why you joined.
> - Inflation is currently 4%. The market situation is better this year.
> - Other workers in similar jobs have recently agreed on a 5% increase.

Salary increase you want:

Other benefits you want:

Training courses you want:

Student B: Manager

> Negotiate the salary increase for one of your employees. Prepare your role carefully before you start.
> - This employee joined the company three years ago.
> - Last year your company made a small loss. All employees (including you) received a salary increase of 3%. Inflation was 5%.
> - This employee has had new responsibilities this year and his/her department has performed well. You want to motivate him/her.
> - Inflation is currently 4%. The market situation is a little better this year.
> - Other workers in similar jobs have recently agreed on a 5% increase.

Salary increase you will offer:

Other benefits you are prepared to pay for:

Training courses you are prepared to pay for:

AIM

To practise dealing with difficult people and conflicts of interest in the context of a teenager/parent negotiation.

TIME

30–40 minutes

PREPARATION

Make one copy of the worksheet for each student in the class.

PROCEDURE

1 Write up on the board the heading *Generation gap*. Elicit the meaning (a difference in attitude, or a lack of understanding, between young people and older people). Ask students if there is a big generation gap between teenagers and parents in their country, and what kinds of things teenagers argue about. Tell the students that they are going to practise a negotiation between a teenager and a parent.

2 Divide the class into pairs and appoint Teenagers and Parents. Give out the correct half of the worksheet to each student. Group together pairs of students with the same role and ask them to prepare ideas together for a few minutes. Circulate and help with vocabulary.

3 Regroup into the A/B pairs who will do the activity. The teenager will start the activity outside the classroom, which is now a living room. The teenagers come into the living room in turn. The parent is sitting down in the living room, perhaps watching t.v. Start the activity, circulate and make a note of good/bad language use.

4 Hold a short feedback slot.

5 (Now, or in the next-class) The As and Bs change roles and repeat the activity. Hold another short feedback slot.

ADDITIONAL GROUP ROLE-PLAY

Instructions to students: Next month you are going away for a week's holiday together, all expenses paid. You have to go together. Decide where you are going to go.

PROCEDURE

1 Divide class into three groups and give them these roles (e.g. on a piece of paper):
   Group A. You all like relaxing on beaches.
   Group B. You all like visiting historic cities, museums and art galleries.
   Group C. You all like active, outdoor holidays such as walking in the mountains.

2 Each group meets separately and decides where it wants to go.

3 The whole class comes together and decides where to go.

Student A: Teenager

> You need to borrow your parents' car next Saturday to go out for the day with some friends. Persuade your parent to let you have the car.

- You are really looking forward to the trip which has been planned for some time. You haven't asked your parents before now because one of your friends was going to take his car, but unfortunately it's not working and is being repaired.
- The last time you borrowed the car a small mark appeared on the door while it was parked. You offered to pay but your parents refused.
- You often wash the car and your parents appreciate this. Next Sunday you are free and can wash the car.

Student B: Parent

> Think of one aspect of your son/daughter's behaviour that you are not happy with and want to talk to him/her about: _____ .

- Next Saturday afternoon you have planned a visit to your parents (your son/daughter's grandparents). You want your son/daughter to go with you, but you haven't told him/her yet. Your parents are getting quite old and they asked especially to see your son/daughter this time.
- Your son/daughter keeps asking to borrow your car. You don't like this. The last time it came back with a small mark on the door. You had to pay, of course.
- Very occasionally your son/daughter offers to clean your car for you, which you appreciate very much. Next Sunday would be a good day for him/her to clean the car.

AIM

To provide a framework for practising a real-life negotiation of the student's own choice.

TIME

variable

PREPARATION

Make one copy of the worksheet for each student in the class.

Consider which of the two procedures below you will use.

PROCEDURE (INDIVIDUAL HOMEWORK)

1 Tell students that they are going to write a short dialogue based on a typical real-life negotiation that they have in their job.

2 Give out a copy of the worksheet to every student. Remind them that they should personalize the dialogue as much as possible. Ask them to write the dialogue for homework and bring it to the next lesson.

3 In the next lesson collect in the dialogues and correct them.

4 (Option) Leave one of the dialogues uncorrected, and photocopy one copy of this for each student. In the next lesson ask students to try to correct/improve this dialogue in pairs. In feedback listen to all the suggestions for reformulations and discuss with the class which is the best. Build up the reformulated dialogue on the board line by line. As a round up, practise reading the new dialogue aloud in open/closed pairs, focusing on pronunciation.

ALTERNATIVE PROCEDURE (CLASSWORK)

1 Tell students that they are going to write a short negotiating dialogue together in pairs. Use any negotiation where both students can predict the content. For example:
  – one of the role-plays from this/another book, before doing it as a fluency exercise
  – one of the role-plays from this/another book, after doing it as a fluency exercise
  Note that it is not necessary to write the dialogue with the same partner who was/will be involved in the role-play.

2 Give out a copy of the worksheet to every student. Divide the class into pairs. Explain that the pair will think of and write the dialogue together, and that both students should keep a record of the whole dialogue. Set a time limit for the task (e.g. 30 minutes). Start the activity and circulate.

3 Ask the pairs to practise reading their dialogues together quietly. Then ask the best pair/s to read out their dialogues for the class.

4 (Option) Take the written dialogues from each pair and redistribute them (so the pairs remain the same but they have another pair's dialogue). First ask the students to study their new dialogues together quietly and make sure they can read them. Then ask them to practise reading the dialogues aloud.

Write a short dialogue using the model below.

Customer		**Supplier**
Ask and answer questions about quantities and price.	◀ ▶	Ask and answer questions about quantities and price.
Ask and answer questions about delivery and terms of payment.	◀ ▶	Ask and answer questions about delivery and terms of payment.
Negotiate: make proposals and react. Link issues.	◀ ▶	Negotiate: make proposals and react. Link issues.
Ask for a final concession.	◀ ▶	Agree. Summarize. Close the negotiation.

_____

_____

_____

_____

_____

_____

_____

_____

_____

_____

_____

_____

_____

_____

_____

_____

_____

_____

_____

_____

_____

_____

_____

Macmillan Education
Between Towns Road, Oxford, OX4 3PP
A division of Macmillan Publishers Limited
Companies and representatives throughout the world

ISBN 978 0 333 99096 4

First published 1999

Designed by: D & J Hunter Book Design and Production

Author's acknowledgments

I would like to thank Dr. Amandio Da Fonseca and all the staff at Egor, Portugal for giving me the opportunity to work inside their company and develop early versions of this material 1993–95. Special thanks to Fernanda Moura, Ana Cardoso and Vera Duque. I would also like to thank Denise Cripps and Chris Hartley for initial interest at Heinemann.

Thanks to all my colleagues at the International House Executive Centre, London for comments and support. In particular, I would like to thank Joe Wiersma, Maurice Cassidy and Lin Coleman for giving me a free hand to pilot activities in class, and the following for specific comments: Andy Goodhall, Nick Hamilton, Violet Jacobsen, Pam Jenkins, Charles Lowe, Rupert Martin-Clark, Dina Serra and Dominique Vouillemin.

Finally, I am grateful to Erica Hall and Mike Sayer for invaluable copy editing and suggestions, and to Karen Spiller, Sarah Curtis, Celia Bingham and Angela Reckitt at Macmillan Heinemann ELT for seeing everything through to completion.

Printed in Thailand

2013 2012 2011 2010 2009
12 11 10 9 8